THE Unapologetic Introvert

It's Time to Unlock Your Quiet Power and Thrive

BRENDALYN CARPENTER PLAYER

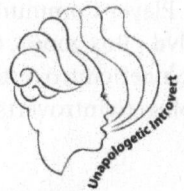

Brendalyn Player Communications
Clarksville, Tennessee

Copyright © 2024 by Brendalyn Carpenter Player

All rights reserved.

First Edition, 2024

Published in the United States by Brendalyn Player Communications.

No part of this book may be reproduced, by any means, without written permission from the author and/or Brendalyn Player Communications. Requests for permission to reproduce material from this work should be sent to 2031 Wilma Rudolph Blvd., Box 30092, Clarksville, TN 37040.

ISBN-13: 979-8-9912543-0-4

Cover Design by Erica Trout Creative
Book Interior Design by Shana Thornton
Author photo by Erica Trout Creative

Library of Congress Control Number: 2024915906

Brendalyn Player Communications
2031 Wilma Rudolph Blvd., Box 30092, Clarksville, TN 37040
https://unapologeticintrovertspace.com/
info@unapologeticintrovertspace.com

10 9 8 7 6 5 4 3 2 1

Disclaimer

The publisher and author provide this book and its contents on an "as is" basis without warranties of any kind. The content of this book is for informational purposes only and is not intended to substitute professional advice or counseling. This book offers personality insights, strategies, and resources based on general observations and research. The effectiveness of these may vary among individuals. If you experience distress related to any aspect of your personality, please consult a licensed health care professional. Anecdotes and examples in this book are modified to protect privacy. Readers acknowledge that the author and publisher are not responsible for actions taken based on the information provided. By reading *The Unapologetic Introvert*, you agree to this disclaimer and its terms.

Dedication

This book is dedicated to my children Arin, Darren, Stehvan, and my daughter-in-love, Nicole. You are my most precious gifts from God. I am deeply honored and grateful to be your Mom. I have learned so much about life just watching you live—fully, freely, and out loud. To my husband, Gregory, who holds my right hand firmly with the most loving and tender grasp, only God could have given you the intuition, the words, and the capacity to melt my heart and calm my muscle spasms. I will dance with you from here to eternity.

Acknowledgements

To my children—Arin, Stehvan, and Darren—you are my inspiration and motivation to step outside my comfort zone each day in pursuit of the vision for our family.

To the mentors and coaches whose wise counsel continues to guide me, I am deeply grateful that you challenge me to my next level.

To dear friends, I cherish every kind word, Saturday coffees, lunches, and dinners, in which we have shared our hearts and hopes. Thank you for your support and prayers.

To leaders, managers, and supervisors, thank you for investing in your introvert team members, for nurturing their nature and leveraging their unique qualities in your organization.

To my fellow introverts, thank you for joining me on this journey. I see you. I pray that a word, sentence, or chapter resonates and empowers you to step into your true nature authentically.

Lastly, I must acknowledge the introvert experts, thought leaders, and laypersons. Thank you for amplifying our voices, as well as translating and elevating the power of introversion. Through your research, books, articles, blogs, videos, and podcasts, I found confidence in my quiet nature. I found my tribe.

I will praise You, for I am fearfully and wonderfully made. Marvelous are Your works, and that my soul knows very well. —Psalm 139: 14 NKJ

"You don't need permission to be you; you just need courage." —Brendalyn Carpenter Player

Contents

Introduction i

Part I
Childhood – The Foundation of a Developing Personality

Chapter 1: If I can't be normal,
　　　　　　I'll be invisible..1

Chapter 2: Small acts of courage
　　　　　　have profound impacts 11

Part II
Transition from Living on Instinct to Living with Intention

Chapter 3: The choice to stand-out
　　　　　　over the struggle to fit in 18

Chapter 4: Unmasking: You'll be surprised
　　　　　　to know I'm an introvert............................. 36

Chapter 5: Strategies to unleash
　　　　　　your inner power and thrive..........................50

Part III
Finding Courage to Be Yourself from the Inside Out

Chapter 6: The Blessing of Discomfort 75

Chapter 7: Embrace your power 86

**Chapter 8: Dear Introvert: Fill your
space unapologetically** 95

Prominent introverts 104
Personality Tests 107
Bibliography 109
About the Author 111

THE
Unapologetic
Introvert

It's Time to Unlock Your
Quiet Power and Thrive

Introduction

As a little girl, I preferred being quiet. Quiet was comfortable like a warm blanket on a damp and cloudy day. Quiet helped me avoid the nervous, queasy feeling introverts get when we are the center of attention.

My inner voice pleaded with those around me, "Don't look my way. Don't call on me. And please don't sit next to me with the expectation of striking up a conversation."

My self-talk was ever present. I heard it in my elementary classroom and at friends' birthday parties, and later, at conference tables and networking events. It protected me from experiencing rejection over my shortcomings and awkwardness.

With thoughts flooding my mind, undermining me and pushing me into the paradoxical safety of insecurities: "I'm not quick and witty. I won't say the right thing at the right time. I'm not sure whether to stand here or sit over there, and I will nearly always choose wrong." It was so much easier to be ... quiet.

Quiet was a safe space. Quiet was where I wanted to be ... until the day came that it wasn't.

I was so firmly grounded in my introversion and the associated personality traits that I didn't recognize a gradual shift taking place in the mental walls I had built and fortified.

I think it's important to pause here to briefly discuss why I've chosen to separate introversion and associated personality traits. According to research (a list of which you'll find in a section at the end of this book), introversion and extroversion are temperaments. Numerous studies have indicated that our brains are neurologically wired from our very beginnings; in other words, we are born with our temperaments.

In the book, *Quiet: The Power of introverts in a World that Can't Stop Talking*, author Susan Cain discusses the "biological origins of temperaments." There is a well-documented difference between our temperament and our personality. Temperament is biologically based behavioral and emotional characteristics that we are born with. Our personalities develop over time and are influenced by external factors. "Some say that temperament is the foundation and personality is the building" (Cain, 2012).

Our temperament reflects the natural manner in which we respond to our environments and our innate preferences. Generally, personality traits are very closely associated, and in many cases, considered one in the same. The major difference between the two is that our personalities can be influenced by our environment, our parents, our families, our communities, and life experiences. If our personalities can be influenced by external factors, it stands to reason that we have the ability to make adjustments in our favor. Only recently, I was able to make the distinction between the two, and doing so helped me peel back layers of negative behavioral conditioning and self-imposed limitations.

From the outside looking in, I was living my best life in the summer of 2021. I was recently re-married and my three adult children—a daughter and twin sons—were living independently and building their own careers. I was

INTRODUCTION

a college-educated, senior-level, strategic communications professional.

My husband and I, both empty nesters, met while enjoying our hobby, more like a passion, for a form of ballroom dancing called Chicago Style Stepping. We traveled across the country, dancing the weekends away. I discovered in my late forties that something unexpectedly beautiful happened when I danced. The mixture of musicality and physical movement combined with my sheer will forced my body to override the brain damage I suffered during infancy. I smiled widely, beaming with joy each time I executed a move and in my mind, saying, "Winning!" Plus, the technique and discipline required to execute the moves aligned with my introvert preference for structure. I was hooked. It's one of the few social experiences I enjoyed.

Every now and then, I'd feel a familiar stomach churn. It ebbed and flowed depending on my environment but never went away completely. More and more, I felt out of sync. *What was this?* I was too busy proving I was good enough in all areas of my life to devote any energy to the occasional distraction.

Like blurred vision slowly coming into focus, I started measuring the true cost of the boundaries I had set. My urges to be seen and heard came more frequently and lingered to the point that I became frustrated when I was ignored or talked over. At times, I felt marginalized in the professional arena, and I stifled the urge to react when being dismissed. Personality traits, which I had mastered to keep me safe in my environment, now betrayed me and felt suffocating.

I observed the people around me as they moved confidently to their own rhythm and pace. I envied their easy banter in social settings, how skillfully they processed information and confidently they expressed themselves. What seemed effortless for them most certainly produced stress and anxiety for me. I got through it, painfully.

> **This book is for those who, like me, feel pressure to ignore our introvert preferences, especially when they conflict with our professional and personal responsibilities.**

This book is for those who, like me, feel pressure to ignore our introvert preferences, especially when they conflict with our professional and personal responsibilities. We prioritize other's needs above our own. We ignore feeling awkward in social settings. Instead, we just push through it. We resist being the first to speak-up, even when we are certain about our answers. Worrying that our quiet nature will be perceived as a deficiency, we over-perform in areas having the least relevance and, as a result, feel undervalued in the workplace. We mask our introversion with extrovert behaviors. After that, we're exhausted by it all.

We want more for ourselves. We crave a different way of being, one that allows us to be seen and heard on our terms, one in which we expose our introversion as confidently as our extrovert counterparts. And yet, how do we get from where we are to where we want to be?

INTRODUCTION

This book follows my journey from habitually shrinking back and playing small to making the space to showcase and celebrate my introvert nature. I share the strategies I used to thrive in environments that drained my energy. You'll learn how to purposefully engage others and share your thoughts with confidence. You'll discover ways to strengthen your presence, impact, and influence.

Peeling back layers to get to the core of my temperament and behaviors, I took accountability and responsibility for the mindset that conditioned me to live small. I share my turning point—how I finally broke free to live without fear of exposure. I silenced the negative self-talk that said, "I can't." And, I developed the courage to champion my authenticity.

Taking those first steps, the self-assessment, meant I had to look honestly at the experiences that shaped my thinking, my behavior, and my choices. Everyone has life experiences that are beyond their control. What we do with those experiences is on us. At some point, we must take action with the parts we can control. We must take responsibility and make deliberate choices to truly live our best life. This is hard work, no doubt, but the reward at the end is a life of purpose and intention. For me, it's what I call having my inside finally match my outside—to be unapologetically me.

In the chapters that follow, I offer resources, tools, and strategies that helped me to break free. I share how to convert perceived challenges into opportunities that move you forward. My hope is that these pages will motivate you to do your work, to take impactful action steps, chart your path, and stay the course to your authenticity.

Together, we will explores the price we pay for living small and the possibilities available to us when we resist

v

the negative impacts of our environment, follow our instincts, and showcase our value. I pray that in reading the pages that follow you will be inspired to push past boundaries, crush fear, become fully present, and deliver the fullest expression of yourself.

How to read this book:

We all read books differently. Some prefer cover to cover, while others start from the back. To improve your experience, the chapters are arranged so those who choose can go directly to the section that is of most interest.

Part 1, the first two chapters, lays a foundation. Through my childhood experience, the reader observes how patterns of behavior, environments, and circumstances influence our developing personalities. I hope you gain insight that will motivate you to consider the ingredients of your unique personality.

Part 2, which includes chapters three through five, offers a deeper dive into the complexities of temperament on the spectrum of introversion to extroversion. It follows my journey along with examples of others who thrive and struggle in the introvert space. Interspersed are practical strategies to help build confidence in expressing your authentic introverted self in various social and professional settings.

The final chapters, six through eight, reflect transformation, the process of moving from self-awareness and self-acceptance to taking personal control, discarding limiting beliefs, and courageously stepping into quiet power—the freedom to be an unapologetic introvert. However you choose to read it, I pray you find value, and I am honored that you are here.

Enjoy your journey!

Chapter 1

If I can't be normal, I'll be invisible

"If you're always trying to be normal, you will never know how amazing you can be." — Maya Angelou

I'll never forget the day Dad finally said, "Yes." It was a typical Wednesday afternoon when my cousin, Willie Cole, stopped by our home on Chicago's south side. He was Dad's nephew and at least thirty years older than me. He seemed more like my uncle than my cousin. Dressed in a shiny, retro-green three-piece suit and wearing a matching brim with a feather in the band, he delivered the '70's flare. I loved listening to him talk. I marveled at his confidence. Words rolled off his tongue with ease and, surprisingly, absent of the southern accent from his Alabama roots. His command of the English language was a talent he employed well in Christian evangelism. He visited regularly, chatting up Dad about family happenings interspersed with a little preacher talk.

Brother Cole was a member of a Pentecostal church located about three blocks away from our house. His visits usually ended with an invitation to church that Dad always declined.

Dad was a quiet man. He was very intelligent. If he didn't know something or how to do something, he would find a way to learn it and master the thing. He was the epitome of a provider for our family that included Mom, my three older sisters, and two younger brothers. Mom worked at home and just as hard as Dad did making a living outside. I marveled at all she accomplished in a day. She knew how to stretch a budget. She made every meal from scratch, and she sewed our clothes when necessary. She was all-in-one—smart, quick-witted, sassy, and very beautiful. She dressed with style and carried herself in a way that exuded confidence. Together, Mom and Dad provided a modest lifestyle. They were careful spenders, and we always had what we needed.

Dad was a constant worker. After working the nightshift at Ford Motor Company, he'd come home, get a few hours' sleep, and then wake back up to work on projects around the house. There was always something that needed fixing or building. He tore down and rebuilt a garage, added a second-floor bathroom, and built a bedroom over the back porch. He did the maintenance and repairs on our cars and those of relatives and neighbors. He believed in using everything inside and around him that had potential. Refusing to allow anything to waste, he made wine from the concord grapevine in our backyard. The garbage men loved when Dad gifted them with a bottle of wine at Christmas time.

I relished the weekends. Every now and then, I'd catch Dad lying on the bed, reading. Sometimes it was the Bible, others it was a tract or pamphlet from the Jehovah's witnesses, and at other times a magazine or newsletter with Elijah Muhammad on the cover. I sensed that he was exploring religion, but he hadn't yet set his mind to one in

CHAPTER 1: IF I CAN'T BE NORMAL, I'LL BE INVISIBLE

particular. Until now, we had gone to church mainly on holidays or special occasions.

That Wednesday that Brother Cole stopped by changed our lives and changed me forever.

I was close enough to Dad to hear the conversation.

"M.B., we're having a revival this week at the church. We have a guest Evangelist who is a faith healer," Brother Cole said.

"You should bring Brenda down to the church and put her in the prayer line."

That's all I heard. I didn't hear Dad's response and didn't know what a faith healer was. All I understood was I could be healed.

I recall carefully studying the baby pictures of me at about two-years-old. I looked normal. Then around three-years-old, my right hand began to twist inward and spasm until my fingers curled into a fist. For years, Mom explained to people who asked that the doctor said I would grow out of it.

When I turned eighteen, I found two neurologists who evaluated me and returned a diagnosis of cerebral palsy. I had suffered a stroke. They couldn't pinpoint when, but sometime during infancy. The stroke caused involuntary muscle spasms on my right side, most noticeably in my right hand and arm. Even now, the spasms never fully go away, but at times, in certain areas, they temporarily relax.

I was nine that Wednesday afternoon—the first time I felt hope that I could be made whole. As evening approached, I begged Dad to take me to church. I told him I wanted to receive prayer from the faith healer. He hadn't planned to go. Finally, he said, "yes" and the two of us went to the revival.

I don't remember the service, the songs, or the sermon. I only remember the prayer line. I remember waiting for my turn to receive prayer. As we inched forward, I could hear people shouting praises, dancing, and crying for joy. My anticipation grew with each outburst.

Finally, I was standing with Dad in front of the evangelist, an older woman with a tall, thin frame. Someone dabbed their finger in olive oil and made the shape of a cross on my forehead. She cupped her hand around my tight fist and began rubbing it as she prayed. Soon others joined in. When my fingers relaxed and began to stretch open, the church erupted in a frenzy of praise and shouting as if I was healed. Dad hugged me so tightly. It was the first time I had ever seen him so emotional.

Back home that night, Dad described the experience to Mom. Dad also received prayer for a back injury that left him in near-constant pain. He described how, after receiving prayer, the pain left his body almost instantly. He snapped the fingers of both hands as he said, "All of a sudden, the pain was gone." He bent his knees, bouncing up and down as he told the story. The next night the entire family went to church. By the end of the revival, several of us were baptized, and we became active members of the church, rarely missing Sunday, Wednesday, and Friday services.

The story of the prayer line was told near and far for the next several years. It felt like every time a faith healer was in town, I was put in the prayer line. By my early teens, even local ministers would call me out of my seat

CHAPTER 1: IF I CAN'T BE NORMAL, I'LL BE INVISIBLE

for prayer. It was always the same experience. My hand would relax, fingers would extend, not all the way but enough for the ministers and church members to give thanks and praises for my healing. Each time, I went home feeling the same as my fingers curled back into a fist and the spasms returned.

The healing I imagined never happened in the prayer line. Instead, I perceived God's answer to my petition, over and over again, was "No." What was worse, I experienced this publicly in front of a congregation that kept encouraging me to pray for my healing. I felt exposed in a way that made me uncomfortable. My nine-year-old mind didn't have the capacity to understand what was happening or to process how it made me feel. By the time I was eighteen, I grew resentful of the prayer line. I felt I had become sport for preachers who wanted to test their anointing in front of their congregations. I didn't want another prayer for healing.

I wanted to tell those well-meaning Christians, who quoted scriptures and admonished me, to keep believing for my healing, to leave me alone. Still, I did as I was told. I memorized and prayed the scriptures. "Have faith in God ... for whosoever shall say unto this mountain, 'Be thou removed, and be thou cast into the sea,' and shall not doubt in his heart, but shall believe that those things which he saith shall come to pass, he shall have whatsoever he saith. Mark 11:22 and 23.

This intensified my feelings of inadequacy, thinking to myself I was, simply, not good enough. *If God's word said He will heal me, then why am I not healed? Do I lack the proper amount of faith? Why am I not worthy of receiving my healing?*

Having no answers to my questions and no comfort for my feelings of rejection, I turned inward. I sought solace inside myself and disconnected from the external. I tried to make myself small and invisible. Although I had no clue of my temperament at the time, my introverted nature provided the safety and comfort I needed then. At least, I could experience a different life in my mind. There, I didn't have to see the faces of people or catch their gaze as they looked at me.

I began to avoid situations that would draw attention to me. I hid my hand as much as I could, under my desk, in my pocket, behind the book I was reading. I refused activities that risked exposure and even stopped playing during recess. I watched as my classmates ran freely around the playground playing games like patty cake and double-dutch. Eventually, I figured out that the less social I became, the safer I felt.

Recalling this childhood experience was difficult, but important. In doing so, I discovered the source of behavioral patterns that I carried into adulthood. I identified triggers and coping mechanisms that at the time made me feel safe and, later, made me feel stifled. I discovered why I felt a push-pull in my introversion, that I had tucked my feelings of brokenness deep inside. I began to understand how common experiences like making mistakes and recovering from them with ease were instead deeply devastating for me because each instance triggered my feelings of brokenness and rejection. As a result, I leaned into my temperament—the ways in which my introversion could protect me. Understanding this complex mental and emotional dichotomy helped start the process of reprogramming my mind, re-conditioning

CHAPTER 1: IF I CAN'T BE NORMAL, I'LL BE INVISIBLE

myself to sort my feelings differently, and remove self-imposed, restrictive boundaries.

Self-assessment: What experiences impact your thoughts about yourself?

- Give yourself grace. We are not broken people; we were thoughtfully and carefully designed.
- Think back to your childhood, before you were told who you were. What thoughts did you have about yourself?

_____

_____

_____

- From that mindset, what did you think you were capable of doing or being? Allow time to deeply explore that thought.

_____

_____

_____

_____

_____

_____

CHAPTER 1: IF I CAN'T BE NORMAL, I'LL BE INVISIBLE

- Consider one of my favorite quotes, *"It's like we all knew who we were when we were little. We knew our power; it was just second guessed."*—Michelle Obama, Advice for girls battling self-doubt.
  Add one of your favorite quotes about battling self-doubt or share an affirmation here that speaks to your experience:

  _____

  _____

  _____

- Think about and list unique qualities, characteristics, or aspects of your personality.

  _____

  _____

  _____

Reflection: Think back to your childhood.

- List experiences that influenced how you saw yourself:

  _____

  _____

  _____

- How do those factors shape the way you see yourself today?

- What did you do, or how did you condition yourself, to create your own safe spaces?

- If you could share a life lesson with your younger self, what would that be?

Chapter 2

Small acts of courage have profound impact

"You can't connect the dots looking forward; you can only connect them looking backwards. So you have to trust that the dots will somehow connect in your future ... believing that the dots will connect down the road will give you the confidence to follow your heart even when it leads you off the well-worn path, and that will make all the difference."—Steve Jobs

I stayed safe and silent through four years of high school. My days were thoughtfully planned for the least amount of exposure. While my siblings rode the city bus to and from high school, Mom drove me to high school and picked me up every day. I went straight to class. There was little time for socializing with friends. That was intentional. Socializing consisted of too many variables like moving freely, laughing, joking, and playing around. There was too much exposure in those spaces. At school, the only place I felt safe was in the structured setting of the classroom where I could hide my hand in the nearest location—in my pocket, under my desk, or shielded by my book. I also avoided being called on to answer questions or speak in front of the class. If not for homeroom when attendance was taken, I considered myself barely there. I didn't attend before or after school activities. Instead of eating in the cafeteria during lunch hour, I went to the library. I got a doctor's note to excuse me from gym class. In four years of high school, I attended no sports events, dances, or proms.

All I knew, then, was that being quiet was safe. In my safe space, my mind wondered about the possibilities of where I might fit in. Somehow, I mustered the courage to try something new.

In the early 80's, most high schools taught basic job and life skills like typing, home economics, and auto shop. Since most English assignments had to be completed using a typewriter, typing class was standard in student curriculums. I never asked why it had not been assigned to me. Passing through the halls, the clickety-clack of the keys striking the paper on the manual typewriters sounded rhythmic. I peeked into the classroom to see students postured in their seats and working their equipment like musical instruments. I listened for the ding that signaled them to push the lever to the right, move the carriage over, and send the paper up to the next line. Something so normal and routine sounded melodic, but seemed out of reach for me.

Near the end of my freshman year, just as the bell rang and students filed out of the room, hustling to their next class, I entered Mrs. Jackson's typing class. When I felt certain no one else would hear me, I asked, "Mrs. Jackson, can you teach me to type with one hand?"

Mrs. Jackson paused. I imagine that she sensed both the urgency and hope in my tone. The warm gaze of her blue eyes put me at ease.

"I have never done it before, and the school has no books with that type of instruction," she said. "I'll do some

CHAPTER 2: SMALL ACTS OF COURAGE

research over the summer. Come back at the beginning of the school year, and we'll see."

When I returned to Mrs. Jackson's typing class at the start of my sophomore year, she presented me with paper copies of left hand-only keyboard instruction. The pages looked as if she had xeroxed a book at the local library. The copies showed where to place the fingers of my left hand in the center of the keyboard, and which fingers to use to depress the keys. Also, there were exercises that familiarized me with depressing the keys first as letters, then words, then sentences. Mrs. Jackson never enrolled me in her typing class. It was never included on my official transcript. I went during my study period, and I received no credit or grade for it. Each day, I sat in the rear of her regular class and Mrs. Jackson taught me to type with one hand. I had no idea, at the time, how valuable this skill would be in my life and career.

Learning to type prepared me for the next courageous move outside my quiet, safe box. At the end of my sophomore year, I responded to an ad in the local paper inviting high school students to attend a summer news writing program, the Urban Journalism Workshop. I applied and was accepted

The Youth News Service, Youth Communication Chicago, was headed by Catholic nun, Sister Ann Heintz. Her vision was to provide a safe place for Chicago's inner city youth to develop writing and leadership skills.

That summer, I learned how to conduct interviews and write stories for *New Expression*, Chicago's only independent newspaper that was written and published by high school students. By fall, I joined the editorial staff. The following year, I became Editorial Director, assigning stories to other students, editing content, and designing pages.

Ann, as she allowed us to call her, was tough. She treated us like adults in the sense that we were expected to fulfill our responsibilities for weekly production. She demanded proper use of the English language and that we write to the same standards as every other local, adult-ran newspaper in Chicago. She did not mince words. Many days, I went home in tears after receiving her edits on something I wrote. Despite the challenges, I loved the structure. I also marveled at her typing skills. Using only the index fingers of her right and left hands, she typed as fast as my classmates.

This was a safe space for introverts like me. I found that I could maneuver easily in the reporting and news writing environment. In those days, we took notes versus relying on voice recorders. The pen and paper were my safety blankets. Conducting an interview offered the structure that introverts find comforting. Interview questions are like having a written script. Interviews, at the basic level, consist of asking questions, recording answers, and writing the story. This type of interaction allowed me to remain relatively in solitude. At that time, there was no thought for me to establish a connection or relate to my subject-matter expert. Those skills would come later.

Writing for the newspaper, along with strong academics, leveled the field for me. This arena relieved my feelings of inadequacy and inferiority. It boosted my confidence and feelings of self-worth. This is where I fit in and where I wanted to stay.

Self-Assessment: Small acts of courage have profound impact

- From childhood forward, what subtle or overt acts did you take to establish boundaries that nurtured your introversion?

  _____

  _____

  _____

  _____

- Were these actions helpful to you or did they positively or negatively impact you at some time in your future?

  _____

  _____

  _____

- Looking back, connect the dots between your introvert behaviors or coping mechanisms, and how are they present in your life today.

THE UNAPOLOGETIC INTROVERT

_____

_____

_____

- Are there behaviors that no longer serve you or areas in which you would like improvement?

_____

_____

_____

Reflection: What were your earliest memories of displaying introvert personality traits?

_____

_____

_____

_____

_____

- Meditate about your interactions from childhood forward.
- What made you feel out of place?

CHAPTER 2: SMALL ACTS OF COURAGE

_____

_____

_____

- What made you feel you belonged?

_____

_____

When do you feel most valued now? What are you doing at those times?

_____

_____

_____

_____

Chapter 3

The choice to stand out over the struggle to fit in

"To be nobody but yourself in a world which is doing its best, night and day, to make you everybody else means to fight the hardest battle which any human being can fight; and never stop fighting."—e.e. cummings

Books are cherished outlets for introverts. They allow us to experience life without limits—to be and do whatever we imagine. Books were my constant companions growing up.

In addition to having cerebral palsy, I was severely asthmatic. In early childhood, an allergy test revealed that I was allergic to just about everything, including weeds, pollen, dust, smoke, chemicals in aerosols, fish, chocolate, cooking oils, cigarette smoke, animals, and preservatives used in snacks like potato chips. Then, through trial and error, we discovered other triggers like extreme heat and extreme cold. Asthma attacks that led to doctors' visits could result in a few days stay at the hospital and a pile of medical bills.

To avoid the cost and to protect me, my parents insisted that I spend my Chicago summers indoors, in the one bedroom that had a window air-conditioner unit. Since my outside world consisted of way too many, "I can't go here or there" and "I can't do this or that" statements, I filled my days with reading books and living in my imagination. In my mind, I could do and be anything. By my late teens, with asthma attacks significantly managed with medication, my personality was firmly set.

I didn't have a word and didn't know a word existed for my natural desire to be quiet and alone. In high school, I was a voracious reader and a deep thinker. My classmates nicknamed me "the professor." Books were comforting and, at times, a crutch. In certain situations, I used books like people use cell phones and other electronics today—to avoid being social and to signal that I was off limits.

My brain is wired to peer beneath the surface of everything. Sometimes, I can't stop myself from asking just one more question. I recognized later in life that one of my introvert traits is an insatiable desire for details. I wanted to know the answers to Who, What, When, Where, Why, and then some. It doesn't matter if it is immediately relevant to me or not, and I am aware this characteristic can be very annoying to my extrovert friends.

I also inherited a few of my Dad's behaviors. He had the ability to wear down any salesperson to get the best possible price on whatever he desired to purchase. He not only talked them down on the price to the value he thought was fair, but he also required the salesperson to have expert knowledge of the item for sale. I watched and listened as Dad worked a salesperson so long, firing one question after another until salesman #1 tapped out and turned the purchase over to salesman #2, to continue answering questions and try to close the deal. Dad rarely exhausted of asking questions.

I loved spending time with Dad. He did not waste words. If he was speaking, most people acted as if they knew something important was being expressed.

THE UNAPOLOGETIC INTROVERT

Occasionally, I'd try to coax a deeper conversation out of him. Because of my nature to explore beneath the surface, I fed my imagination with my parents' life experiences. Born and raised in rural Alabama in 1938, Dad's mom, Amelia, died when he was four, and his father, Odie, was mostly absent. Dad experienced a life of going to bed hungry and waking up cold. The fourth child of seven siblings, he learned to fend for himself, working the fields as a farm hand and then doing odd jobs until he could save enough money to move to Chicago. I admired his resilience, courage, and determination to make a better life for himself and for his family. I admired his ingenuity, calm demeanor, and generous spirit.

I was born in the late 60s, too young to grasp the political climate of the period in which my family lived. I could only read the accounts about Emmett Till, Malcolm X, Dr. Martin Luther King Jr., and the Civil Rights Movement. I wondered what life was like for my parents. Mom told us how her family hid her oldest brother when night riders came looking for him. I saw pain on her face and tears well in her eyes when she told the story of her father's death. Alfred Ball, my maternal granddad, was a proud man and the son of a White mother and Black father. He had a reputation for being a man of conviction who resisted the intimidation and threats of racist White men in their small Alabama town. Until one day, in 1952, a truck loaded with pulp wood logs mysteriously came unhinged and rolled on top of him. At the funeral home, his Black wife, my grandmother, and Mom, the oldest of her three siblings at that time, were not permitted to see him immediately after his death until his White aunts instructed that he be brought out for the family to view. At 83, I still hear the pain in Mom's voice as she tells the

CHAPTER 3: THE CHOICE TO STAND OUT

story; her hands clasped tightly one over the other, as if to avoid trembling. The question she had at ten-years-old remains unanswered: *How were no visible injuries on his body after befalling a truck load of pulp wood?*

Dad's youthful photo, wearing a Fedora, reminded me of Emmett Till's from the picture in 1955 *Jet* Magazine. Thinking how easily such violence could befall Black people, I struggled to understand feeling normal during a time when the threat of violence and inequitable treatment was the way of life. I recalled the details of their lives over and over in my mind, trying to feel what they could possibly have felt under those circumstances.

Once in a while, I would fire off a few questions in hopes the answers would help me see the experience through their eyes.

"Dad, did you have to drink from the colored faucet?"

"Yes," he said.

"How did it make you feel?" I asked.

"That's how we had to live back then," he replied.

"Why didn't you graduate high school?" I asked.

"I had to make money to eat and have a place to stay," he answered.

"What was it like working in the fields?" I asked.

"It was hard work for a little pay," he said.

"If you could have finished school and had the chance to be anything you wanted, what did you want to be?"

"I think I would have liked to be a lawyer."

Dad answered my questions with certainty. I searched for frustration, even anger in his tone for the hardship he suffered. Instead, I found resolute peace. I observed a person who was self-aware and confident in his abilities. There was neither malice nor resentment for his journey. He found a pathway to a life of relative safety, stability, and a loving home. Absorbing every detail strengthened my inner world. I could stay there in the place of curiosity that led me to be alone for hours on end.

In this space, where my mind and intellect had no limits, I was whole. I also committed to having a strong work ethic. I strived for perfection in every area of my life. I placed a significant burden on myself, believing that overcompensating in those areas was the price for my physical imperfection, the cerebral palsy that, in my nine-year-old mind, God most certainly did not choose to heal.

The first of my family to earn a college degree, I planned for a career that was familiar and safe. I freelanced for the local newspaper during college. Upon graduation, I applied for my first full-time job as a beat reporter at the newspaper. I was so confident during the interview that I didn't see it coming.

"I'm not going to hire you," the editor said. This was the man for whom I had freelanced for the last two years of college, and he chose not to offer me the position.

"You have the ability to do more than beat reporting," he said.

I was devastated about being denied entry into the space I thought was perfect for my introvert nature.

After several more months of job hunting and out of frustration, I accepted an eighteen-month Army Career Training and Development internship. I entered the Army Public Affairs profession, a career track completely the opposite of my personality. I received master's level training to be an Army spokesperson, public information, community relations and media officer.

Instead of a career that aligned with my introverted nature and personality, I worked in one of the most visible, fluid, and routinely high-stress career fields in the

CHAPTER 3: THE CHOICE TO STAND OUT

> **Instead of a career that aligned with my introverted nature and personality, I worked in one of the most visible, fluid, and routinely high-stress career fields in the Army Civilian Corps.**

U.S. Army Civilian Corps. Relying on intellect and my no-defect work ethic, I committed to successfully perform my duties. I considered it an honor to serve the information needs of our soldiers and their families.

In many ways, I discovered that I was perfectly suited for the critical thinking, analytical, and complex problem-solving aspects of my new career. My natural tendency for discretion and attention to detail was an easy fit. Other responsibilities required more energy. I developed the skills necessary to field calls from national media, conduct a press conference, perform crisis communication, escort dignitaries, and advise Army leaders. I paid close attention to mentors who paved the way. One of my first lessons came from a female Lieutenant Colonel and I Corps Public Affairs Officer at, then, Fort Lewis, Washington.

Fresh out of my internship, I watched her movements in the presence of Army commanders, and I marveled at her mastery of authority as a woman in a predominantly male military environment. She had quiet confidence that she used skillfully. "When the situation around you speeds up, you slow down," she advised.

I watched as she stepped up to the podium to answer media questions about the death of a soldier. As she raised her chin, lifted her eyes toward the cameras, and leaned into the microphone, I saw the shift in her demeanor. She delivered empathy, authenticity, and the conviction necessary for the unfortunate circumstances. That lesson formed the playbook of my career.

At times uncomfortable, I fulfilled my duties with my insides balled up in knots. Although I mastered the skills necessary to be successful at every stage in my career, no amount of training could soothe my inner discomfort. Success, at that time, required that I absorb the stress and anxiety of wearing an extrovert persona, while tamping down my introversion.

I found myself acknowledging my introversion only as it pertained to my feelings of inadequacy, the shame and embarrassment for having cerebral palsy. Introversion helped to avoid drawing attention to myself. Then, there were associated personality traits like my penchant for details. In the professional arena, this is often misunderstood as insecurity, lack of trust, or micromanaging. It was none of those. Introverts try to avoid what Olsen Laney calls, "the experience of brain locking." To avoid having a blank moment, we over-prepare by accruing as much information as possible. It was the first time that I read words perfectly describing what I had been feeling for so many years (Laney, 2002).

I discovered the root of that compulsion was fear of being unprepared. The embarrassment of appearing uninformed, or worse, making a mistake, would only confirm the truth I had accepted about my nine-year-old self, that I was broken. I was not good enough. So, I strove for perfection.

Committed to my boundaries, which included staying inside my box, I continued to suppress my true nature. I

CHAPTER 3: THE CHOICE TO STAND OUT

forced a life image that was not truly mine. I devoted myself to over-delivery in all areas of life, or at least trying to overly excel with all that was within my power.

I struggled in extrovert-centric environments. I felt awkward in social or group settings. Then, thinking about feeling odd in the moment only made me feel and appear more uncomfortable.

Perhaps you can relate. Are there times when engaging in conversation, you are frustrated because of a tendency to process before speaking, often losing the moment to interject your thoughts? You rehearsed in your mind what you wanted to say for so long that the conversation moved on to another topic? You regretted waiting so long and the person beside or behind you spoke your words as if they had read your mind?

Protective behaviors I practiced as a little girl betrayed me as an adult professional. At times, I felt undervalued and invisible as if being quiet also implied I had nothing of value to offer. My intellect and work ethic could not overcome an environment that demanded and elevated extrovert personality traits. When entering a conference room, I looked toward the back row rather than the front seat. I chose the open seat along the wall rather than the chair at the conference table. I rarely spoke first, even when I was certain of the answer.

Slowly, I felt the shift occurring inside me. I became dissatisfied with living inside my limiting walls. I wanted to fill the space where I belonged. I wanted to be seen. I wanted to be heard. I just needed to figure out how to get from where I was with my various triggers, where I had conditioned myself to behave, and move to where I wanted to be. I paid more attention those experiences, pushed myself more, but not nearly enough.

I paid little attention to the personality tests we take in the typical leader development courses. The Myers-Briggs Personality Type Indicator, and others like it, delivered the same result. My dominant trait was Introvert. Depending on the year, I floated between the ISFJ and the INFP. Introverted, Sensing, Feeling, Judging personalities are quiet, friendly, responsible, and conscientious. They are committed to meeting their obligations and painstakingly thorough and accurate.

Introvert, Intuitive, Feeling, and Perceiving personalities are idealistic and loyal to their values. They seek congruency between their internal and external lives. They are curious, quick to see possibilities, and can be a catalyst for implementing ideas. INFP's are good listeners, seek to understand people, and help them fulfill their potential (Myers-Briggs Type Indicator).

Renowned psychoanalyst Carl Jung first introduced the concepts of introversion and extroversion. Based on Jung's theory, understanding our personality type should be leveraged in the workplace. The information can help to build teams that perform well together as well as help leaders mentor and develop individual members in ways that make them feel valued and motivate their best performance (Open Extended Jungian Type Scales).

Although informative for the workplace, I didn't dwell on my introversion or my personality traits and preferences or what I needed to feel whole. I remained fixated on covering my flaws, and unfortunately, added introversion to that category.

Personalities are not measures of intelligence or abilities. Research suggests that being a good talker does not always translate to being the best thinker or the smartest person in the room (Cain, 2012). Talkers are seen

CHAPTER 3: THE CHOICE TO STAND OUT

as leaders, gain more attention, and can be perceived as more powerful. Too many times, leaders overlook the critical-thinking and complex problem-solving skills of their employees at the table as they consider the feedback of their more vocal colleagues. The best thing a leader can do is recognize and tap into the value that each employee delivers in their organization. I wish that I had this understanding and self-acceptance years ago. I was a thinker more than a talker.

All types, traits, and preferences comprise unique gifts and qualities. However, I felt introversion was neither celebrated nor recognized as a positive characteristic. It took years for me to understand how my introversion, compounded by my distorted self-image and the coping skills developed as a little girl, influenced every decision of my life. There is adequate space in the workplace for all personalities. However, I lacked the self-awareness, confidence, and tools to properly advocate for myself.

We are all born with unique qualities and have preferences that are swayed by our life experience. For me, living with cerebral palsy influenced the way I interacted with people and how I saw myself in my environment. As a result, I approached a typical project from a different perspective than my teammates. Although I championed my team to excel in their capacities, always brewing underneath, was fear. Inside me, delays, errors, and anything less than perfect exposed the little girl in me who wasn't whole.

I didn't recognize how much energy I was investing in overcompensating for my perceived shortcomings. I was a military spouse who took care of home so that her soldier could focus on his military duties. I followed my mother's example by serving the kids a hot breakfast every day before school. Sundays, I prepared full meals with dessert. I served twenty years at our community church, teaching Sunday School and Vacation Bible School. I shuttled the kids to practices, soccer, volleyball, basketball, and the youth choir and youth usher board. And, I had achieved career success, progressing from an intern to the Director of Public Affairs and leading a team. I had the honor of working at the Department of the Army Pentagon, escorting White House staff, the Secretaries of the Army and Defense, national and international dignitaries, and advising Army leaders.

Yet, nothing made the little girl inside me feel whole. I was naturally an introvert operating under unrealistic, self-imposed limitations. I was over-serving and it was killing me.

Shrinking back was so familiar and automatic. Placing the needs of others over my own was compulsive, comfortable and disturbing at the same time. Relentlessly giving was so deeply engrained it took control of me without resistance. At least my body fell in line, while chaos brewed inside me.

The headaches started in 2021. At first, they were occasional and then they became so consistent that I started taking notes. My body signaled that something was seriously wrong, but I was obsessed with fulfilling my day-to-day activities, personal and professional obligations that I associated with being whole.

"January: The headache started overnight. Took two Excedrin ..."

"April: Headache and now swelling in the back of my neck ..."

"June: Headache, so bad I could not open my eyes. It was blinding. Trip to the ER for stronger meds ..."

CHAPTER 3: THE CHOICE TO STAND OUT

"July: Headache overnight, could not go back to sleep. Two Excedrin ..."

I followed this regimen, pacifying the stress signals month after month and becoming Excedrin dependent in the process.

My moment of clarity came in spring 2023. Memorial Day weekend, a headache started in the center of my forehead. Having the pain so concentrated in that one area was unusual, but I was familiar with having chronic headaches for the past two years. I followed my normal routine and took an Excedrin right away. As I went to bed, I noticed that the pain traveled down the left side of my face. I hoped the meds would work as I pulled the covers around my neck and fell asleep. The next morning, I woke up with a swollen left eye. Looking closer, my eye was not only swollen, but it also appeared to be drooping. By the afternoon, I was in the doctor's office. Days later after multiple MRIs, I learned that I had suffered a stroke. Hearing the doctor say those words, and determining that it was most likely stress related, I was immediately grateful that the impact was minor considering the possibilities.

I occasionally thought of what a second stroke might do to my body. *How debilitating would it be? How might I care for myself if I lost the use of my left arm or hand, or worse?* This health scare became a catalyst for change. Something shifted inside me as I reflected on how much time I spent hiding my introversion instead of embracing it as a strength and living on my own terms. This time, I made a different choice to address my feelings of brokenness and to accept my whole self.

I wanted more for myself and was open to receiving help getting there. My transformation journey included seeking licensed mental health support as well as searching for answers on my own. I vividly remember the day my search landed on Jenn Granneman's website "Introvert, Dear", an online community for introverts.

Reading one article after the other was like immersing myself in a healing sanctuary. I found my tribe, people who have similar preferences—people who celebrate their unique qualities and the power of their introversion.

Inspired, I dove deeper, exploring books by Jenn Granneman and other thought leaders about introversion and personality traits. Their insights opened a new world of self-awareness and self-acceptance.

In *The Secret Lives of Introverts: Inside our Hidden World* (Skyhorse Publishing, 2017), Granneman describes her enlightenment when first learning the word "introvert" and the relief of feeling understood. Reading her work, I felt free to accept my quiet nature as my strength for the first time, but I barely scratched the surface. These authors whom I related to—and their books—Granneman, along with authors Susan Cain of *Quiet* (Crown, 2012) and Marti Olsen Laney of *The Introvert Advantage* (Workman Publishing, 2002), set me on the path to connecting the dots for my life choices, the behaviors that served me, and those that I had the ability discard. Most of all, I gained confidence to proudly display my introversion as the natural gift that it is. I began the healing process of unloading all of my unnecessary baggage and adjusting elements of my personality that no longer served me.

I returned to my office with a new mindset and ready to start my next chapter.

Retiring after twenty years of service, I am proud of my career and thankful for the opportunity to serve our soldiers and their families. I learned a very important lesson—that I did it the hard way. My deep desire to be whole conditioned me to strive for an unrealistically perfect presence. It caused me to work harder than necessary, longer hours than I should have, and accept responsibilities beyond what was required of me. I needed a roadmap to take me from where I was to where I wanted to be.

Does this experience resonate with you? If so, please take it to heart. You don't have to struggle. I discovered that you can live fully on your terms, whether you desire to stand-up, stand out and shine, or prefer to deliver your best performance in the background.

After the stroke, I committed to living differently. I was done hiding. God had given me an opportunity to reset, and I was going to take it. I did this only after receiving what my nine-year-old mind could not comprehend about my experience in the prayer line. That God never said, "No" to my petition. God designed me purposefully for my life and for the people I get to serve.

First, I accepted responsibility for years of forcing myself into a lifestyle that placed other people's preferences above my own. I was guilty of shrinking back when I should have been shining brightly. I ignored God's perfect will for me, His intentionality, and His design for my life.

Now, I had a chance to step outside the box, discover, and live in my truth. I asked myself candidly: *What if I showed up for myself fully, free of embarrassment and shame? What if, in sharing my journey, I can help someone else who is struggling to be whole? What if I shared my quiet power, the habits and quirks that are unique to me? What if I expose my perfect imperfection?*

When I answered those questions, I realized that I can take that seat at the table. I can have that conversation. I can shine brightly in the room. I can display my value. I can be fully present. I can fulfill my assignment, get into the arena, and take my space.

That was my moment. What's yours? Think about your life. Do you recall moments in which you felt God was shifting you? Do you recognize that feeling? When it comes, lean into it. Just past fear, you may feel overwhelming peace and gratitude. This is your special creative space. It's where you commune alone with God.

Let go. Accept your divine design. Be free.

Self-assessment: Considering that every individual has challenges that they are dealing with, I encourage you to assess how your life experiences impact the degree to which you lean into your introversion and the choices you make in your life.

- In what areas do you feel your lifestyle aligns with your introversion? In what areas do you feel out of alignment?

    _____

    _____

    _____

- List at least three steps you could take to bring form to a lifestyle that nurtures your introvert nature:

    _____

    _____

    _____

    _____

THE UNAPOLOGETIC INTROVERT

- What's one nurturing behavior you'll commit to doing, beginning now? Where do you need to take ownership and control?

  _____
  _____

- Are you experiencing relationships, a lifestyle, a career authentically, or checking the box?

  _____
  _____
  _____

Reflection: A Leap of Faith

- What leap of faith are you thinking of taking? Why are you afraid or shrinking back from taking a leap?

  _____
  _____
  _____

CHAPTER 3: THE CHOICE TO STAND OUT

- Is there an opportunity that you regret passing? If so, what was the opportunity and why did it pass?

  _____

  _____

  _____

- What would you do differently with those same options today?

  _____

  _____

  _____

- What's one thing you could do today to better reflect your true self?

  _____

  _____

Chapter 4

Unmasking: "You'll be surprised to know I'm an introvert."

"Don't think of introversion as something that needs to be cured... Spend your free time the way you like, not the way you think you're supposed to."—Susan Cain

At our first meeting, Camille, my new accountant, took her time getting to the numbers. Ignoring my spreadsheets, stacked receipts, invoices, and other random documents, Camille asked, "Tell me what you do and why?"

My side-eye, tilted head, and forehead lines signaled she had interrupted my flow, as I was laser focused on preparing for tax day.

"I like to get to know my clients in a way that I understand their business and can better advise them on setting up their accounting strategy," Camille explained.

I gave her my one-minute pitch. "I help introverts express their unique qualities, communicate with confidence, and deliver value in any environment they choose." As she leaned in, I went a little deeper.

"I help individuals who, at times, feel undervalued and ignored. They are uncomfortable in social settings,

CHAPTER 4: UNMASKING, "I'M AN INTROVERT."

have difficulty speaking in group settings, or gravitate to the back of a room when they really should be up front," I said. I felt my energy rise with each word.

"Humph, some of those apply to me but not all," she said, matter-of-factly. "I used to think I was an introvert, but I'm not. I used to be afraid to speak in public, and I joined Toastmasters to help me get over that." She continued, "When introverts are at social events, they are usually the first to leave, but in the right setting, I'm just getting started. Sometimes I stay so long I end up helping with the clean-up. But I do have difficulty looking people in the eyes when I talk to them."

"That's exactly why I serve," I said. "The spectrum of introversion to extroversion is so broad and our personality traits are so complex that it's challenging for most people in the middle of the spectrum to claim one over the other. However, there is a stigma associated with being an introvert that sometimes makes us feel we must defend our preferences," I said, continuing, "My goal is to help individuals, especially introverts, display their preferences and personalities without fear or feelings of inadequacy."

She nodded, as we both sighed and relaxed in familiar company.

I can't number the times I've had similar reactions. The most common is, "Because of what I do for a living, most people are surprised when I tell them I'm an introvert."

This is true in most workplaces. Some of us are able to tap into traits across the spectrum of introversion to extroversion. We maneuver however necessary for our personal and professional success. We establish boundaries that secure time and space to nurture ourselves and recharge when necessary. There are others, like me, who struggle with feeling guilty or deficient to the degree that we stifle our own needs, or worse, we accept the judgment of others.

As noted in Chapter Three, psychoanalyst Carl Jung is credited with developing the spectrum of introversion to extroversion in the early 1920s. He delved into this study to understand people's natural tendencies, their temperaments, and personality traits. He hoped to use this information to capitalize on an individual's strengths and to mitigate their weaknesses.

Researchers agree about the general temperaments of introverts and extroverts. Introverts are inwardly focused. They draw energy from internal sources. Being social can be depleting. Extroverts are outwardly focused. They draw energy from external sources. Being social is most often energizing. Extroverts in a space of solitude for an extended period might experience a decrease in their energy level.

In 1927, American social scientist Kimball Young coined the term *ambivert*. This is where most of us fall along the spectrum. Ambiverts display varied introvert and extrovert preferences, thereby eliminating the exclusivity of either trait. The spectrum has been further defined to include *introverted extrovert* and *extroverted introvert*. There are a few other commonly used terms that further delineate variance in personality traits along the spectrum, but for simplicity, we'll focus on these.

Although some individuals lean more heavily to one side of the spectrum than the other; according to Jung, there are no pure introverts or pure extroverts.

CHAPTER 4: UNMASKING, "I'M AN INTROVERT."

From my experience and observing the experiences of others, identifying as an introvert can be undesirable. In other words, a negative connotation is more likely associated when introverts express or display their preferences. At times, I felt the need to defend myself against an assumption that my preference to process before speaking presented a deficit in my performance or capabilities. Hence, as discussed in previous chapters, the internal and external pressure drove my tendency to over-perform and to be a perfectionist when it wasn't required of me.

We absorb the negative connotations that are expressed subtly in our environments. We ignore generalizations. If someone is described as a loner, it's more often in association with an unfavorable experience or observed behavior of that individual.

In her book, *Quiet*, Susan Cain asks us to look at the words used to describe introverts and extroverts. Describing someone as "anti-social" draws a different perception than describing them as "differently social," Cain writes. The former strikes a negative tone, while the latter has a neutral tone, neither positive nor negative.

Most of us operate in the ambivert space. We enjoy others, but we need some alone time. We can be outgoing in the right context and environment. We might also work well in teams and individually.

However, we operate in many environments that highlight, praise, and elevate extroverts over introverts. We observe greater value placed on extrovert tendencies versus introvert personality traits. Many of us learn to adopt and display those traits according to our responsibilities.

I am not exploring this line of thinking to harp on disparities, as if societal adjustments offer the sole resolution. I am suggesting that for introverts, without thinking about it, we internalize a deficit, and we choose to operate or modify our behaviors to follow that line of thinking. We create boundaries, box ourselves in, and struggle unnecessarily. We dismiss our nature and live mostly "like" an extrovert.

We perform as required to maintain friendships, to build networks, and to earn a promotion. We do this, while denying our introverted nature. We reserve that for when we are home alone, or maybe not even then. If we live with an extrovert partner, roommate, or children, we are still "on" more hours than we care to be or admit. Those suppressed feelings seep out over time and present in the form of stress, mental health and quality of life issues, career stagnation and dissatisfaction, and strained relationships.

The most important takeaway is that we are all wired differently. The spectrum of introversion to extroversion pertains to our temperaments. In her book, *The Introvert Advantage: How Quiet People Can Thrive in an Extrovert World* (Workman Publishing, 2012), author and researcher, Marti Olsen Laney discusses the genetic influence on temperament: "Temperament begins with genes," Olsen Laney writes. Our temperament is driven by our neuro-chemical activities within our bodies.

Neurotransmitters direct the amount of blood flow along the pathways to brain centers. Laney's book presents a study of the amount of blood flow in the brain and concluded that behavioral differences between introverts and extroverts result from using different brain pathways

CHAPTER 4: UNMASKING, "I'M AN INTROVERT."

that influence where we direct our focus – internally or externally.

Whether extrovert, introvert, or ambivert, both physical and neurological differences exist in every individual. Additionally, as mentioned earlier, life experiences help shape our personalities. Your personality is the combination of qualities that form your unique character. "It's your introversion with your life experience piled on top," Granneman writes.

These differences influence our lifestyle, career choices, relationships, and how we interact. Understanding and accepting our individuality generates confidence. Instead of measuring a perceived deficit, we can highlight our unique capabilities and the value that we deliver in our environment.

In processing my own experience and immersing myself in the research of experts and thought leaders on the subject of introversion, I have observed three categories of introverts that I have named and defined as follows: Absolute introverts, adopters, and adapters.

The categories reflect the degree to which introverts operate comfortably in their preferences and thrive in their environments. Absolute introverts are the standard bearers of introverts; adopters tend to do what others want; and adapters can fall anywhere along the spectrum.

Absolute introverts are the most accepting of themselves. They are self-aware and most likely to choose lifestyles, careers, and relationships that align with their personalities. They are vocal about what they like and don't like and set boundaries to protect their preferences. These are our friends who decline an invite to an event or social gathering without any feelings of guilt. They'll excuse themselves from an activity when they've reached their point of overstimulation. They rarely exhaust themselves for the sake of appearances. They are fully comfortable asking for what they need and making choices that align with their own desires. They will accept discomfort for only short periods and will quickly find ways to reshape their circumstances to their benefit. They fully embrace their personalities without fear, guilt, shame, or regret.

Adopters choose the preferences of others over their own. They may operate at a level or in a space in which they are uncomfortable for the sake of personal or professional responsibilities. They are more often in careers that consistently challenge their introversion. Rather than own their choices and develop skill sets that will help them thrive and shine brightly, they operate out of obligation. Often, the stress of the experience leads to missed opportunities and fear of failure or being perceived as deficient. These individuals feel compelled to over-perform and over-deliver. We're exhausted from our own self-talk that we are not enough.

Adapters appear engaged, interactive, action-oriented, direct, and willing to be problem-solvers. They appear to move about confidently. They speak up when the opportunity presents itself and don't hesitate when the time comes to take center-stage. They are our friends who, after several minutes of captivating dialogue, will say, "I'm actually an introvert." These individuals operate in their extrovert-centric environments with the least amount of resistance. They spend the necessary time to be fully "on." Then, they make space to turn "off," nurture themselves, and allow their energy to replenish.

CHAPTER 4: UNMASKING, "I'M AN INTROVERT."

Adapters appear to be comfortable in whatever space they find themselves. They've learned to manage the stress of an overly stimulating environment and to delay the gratification of solitude for the time being. Adapters operate in the flow of personality traits from introversion to extroversion. They are able to perform at the level necessary within their environment. While they have a much higher threshold for comparisons, they still carry a tinge of guilt over not being as direct as their extrovert friends or co-workers. Because they are generally the easy-going, respectful, stay-in-your-lane type, adapters may excuse the mistreatment of others as a factor of their personality: *I'm just a nice person. Our supervisor wouldn't have even tried that with Sheila*, an outspoken extrovert. Although adapters have found a medium in which they can operate, it is occasionally "unhappy" because they must revisit challenges similar to adopters.

Numerous books, articles, studies, and tests are available to help you understand your preferences and personality traits that may fall anywhere on the spectrum of introversion to extroversion. I encourage you to do your own research. Take a couple of personality assessments. You'll discover there is no absolute answer. No document, research, or article can pinpoint your unique characteristics. Your personality is just that. Yours. There are no two alike. There are similarities. There are generalities, but no one has your exact temperament.

What's beautiful is that no other human being can make the contribution that you were created, designed, and equipped to deliver in your time on Earth. So, when you consider your personality, your introversion, use this book and your own research as a guide to give you clarity.

Also, trust yourself. Nobody can tell you more about yourself than you can. Spend time on self-reflection. Consider the ways in which you like to communicate, the ways in which you like to interact and engage, as well as the things that feed you and the things that don't.

Personality traits among introverts and extroverts can be fluid, especially among those who identify as ambivert. You may consider yourself an introvert but disagree with one or more preferences. For example, you may not enjoy a day of solitude. You may be an introvert who is not completely drained after a social event, or you may be an extrovert who craves longer periods of solitude.

I enjoy silence. Complete silence for me is not silent at all because my internal conversation is constant. Silence gives me the space to focus, organize, and convert thoughts to actions.

Now, I understand why my environment feels chaotic when I have to split my attention. I recognize the anxious, unsettled feeling when talking on a cell phone while music is playing, the television is blaring, or people are conversing in the background. It's too much stimulation.

Before I began paying attention to what I was feeling, the inner chaos was something I managed. I coped. I made do while ignoring my own needs. Similarly, stores that have rows upon rows of clothing that you have to painstakingly weed through to find your style, size, color, and fit are exhausting. When it's crowded and the line wraps around and back three times like an airport luggage check-in, I'm done.

Is every introvert like that? No. That's me recognizing my introversion and making the necessary accommodations. Instead of ignoring my physiological responses, I pay attention as they inform me. Now, I am

CHAPTER 4: UNMASKING, "I'M AN INTROVERT."

equipped to express what I need or set boundaries. Identifying my quirks—what disrupts or supports my well-being—allows me to be more selective with my environment.

Self-awareness and the courage to address your needs gives introverts a level of control and comfort to excel on your terms. Discovering and setting boundaries is the equivalent of saying, "I choose me."

Self-assessment: I discovered the kind of space that I need to be productive, like operating in silence is impactful. What is it for you?

_____

_____

- What are the actions, thoughts, and ideas that position you for peak performance?

  _____

  _____

- What are the distractions that prevent you from peak performance?

  _____

  _____

  _____

CHAPTER 4: UNMASKING, "I'M AN INTROVERT."

- List 1-3 of your unique characteristics, preferences, or quirks?

  _____

  _____

  _____

- Do external factors enhance or disrupt your quality of life?

  _____

  _____

  _____

- Do you set boundaries that protect your well-being?

  _____

  _____

  _____

Reflection: Observations of personality traits and strategies

- During her first interaction with Camille, what personality trait(s) did you observe in Brendalyn?

47

THE UNAPOLOGETIC INTROVERT

_____
_____
_____

- What personality traits did you observe in Camille?

_____
_____
_____

- Why do you think Camille shared that she wasn't an introvert?

_____
_____
_____

- What strategies did Camille use to enhance her confidence and nurture her personality?

_____
_____
_____

CHAPTER 4: UNMASKING, "I'M AN INTROVERT."

- List a strategy you use or could use in your own environment.

    _____

    _____

    _____

    _____

    _____

Chapter 5

Strategies to unleash your inner power and thrive

"And the day came when the risk to remain tight in a bud was more painful than the risk it took to blossom."— Anaïs Nin

The morning of her organization's annual report luncheon, Jeri is feeling it. Stomach cramps signal it's time to get up from a restless night, and she heads for the bathroom. Nerves and anxiety always give her an upset stomach before a big event. Once dressed, the click of her heels, as she moves back and forth across the hardwood floor, stirs her husband and he rolls over adjusting his position in bed. He's used to the nervous energy and knows to let it run its course. Arriving at work, there's no time for small talk. Jeri's on a deadline; she had the most difficult time finishing the employee newsletter. She completed the draft days ago, but today nothing flowed or made sense.

As she sits through two meetings, Jeri tries to stay attentive, taking copious notes, so she's prepared to back-brief her supervisor. The whole time she's thinking about the annual employee luncheon in two hours: *How can I get*

CHAPTER 5: STRATEGIES TO UNLEASH INNER POWER

out of going to the luncheon? Do I really need to be there? What if I don't go? Will my absence give the impression that I'm not a team player? I work with these people every day, should I be obligated to spend my lunch hour, really ninety minutes, chatting them up, too? she wondered. *I have so much work to do, and this will only put me farther behind. Well, I have been talking about a lateral shift from marketing to the HR department,* she reasoned. *I wonder if my absence will hurt my chances of competing for that open position.*

Stomach cramping and aggravated by coworkers interrupting while she makes the final edits, she emails the newsletter to her supervisor just in time and departs for the luncheon stopping by the bathroom on the way. *I'll show my face, sit near the back, and pray to be left alone.*

The previous chapters laid a foundation for understanding the difference between introvert and extrovert personality traits. In those chapters, I asked you to identify how you see yourself along the spectrum. I guided you into taking responsibility for the habits and behaviors that prevent you from being fully expressive.

This chapter will discuss strategies that will help you move toward your goal of becoming more confident in your introvert space.

Strategy #1: Master yourself in the environment

I initially titled this strategy, "Master your environment," but the truth is that we are often in environments we cannot control. Introverts typically experience stress and anxiety in these spaces. Hence, Strategy #1 is titled "Master *yourself* in the environment."

The most important thing we must do is self-assessment. I did this as I was preparing to transition out of federal service. This is common when individuals are moving out of one season into another. I read similar accounts of other individuals who were recently retired or retiring.

In the article, "10 Survival Tips for Introverted Leaders," author Steve Friedman recounts his thirty-year career as an introverted leader working for Shell Oil: "Though I treasured many of those relationships, the level of conflict and the call for thinking on my feet exhausted me daily. During my tenure, I certainly did learn more about who I was... I realized I'm an introvert." Friedman recounts the difficulties he faced as an introvert leader, identifying the tools that showcase the value of his quiet nature in the corporate environment.

He detailed the true cost of taking the fake it 'til you make it approach: "Through grit, determination, and a high personal cost, I climbed the corporate ladder. However, my stress level went through the roof. As a result, my health degraded, and I sought destructive means of coping with the stress, through binge eating and drinking," Friedman said.

Upon reading this, I let out a sigh of relief knowing that I'm not the only one.

CHAPTER 5: STRATEGIES TO UNLEASH INNER POWER

I agree with Friedman that we should not place blame on our employer when we struggle or feel like an outsider in our workplaces. It is our responsibility to "embrace our introversion and find contentment."

I say, "Don't wait to reflect on your accomplishments and actions you wish you had taken. Start today. Make self-assessment a routine rather than checking a box at a transition point. Use self-evaluation to measure your progress in the direction of achieving your goals."

Do your introvert preferences align with your lifestyle, personal or professional responsibilities, and career goals?

Let's look at Jeri for example. Jeri's an introvert who prefers structure. Arriving to work on time, she focuses on getting to her desk, checking emails and her calendar, and then returning missed calls from the previous day. Then, Jeri gets to work. Checking off her to-do list as the day progresses; the more checked boxes, the more accomplished she feels at the end of the day. She's competent and, for the most part, enjoys her job. However, she has social anxiety. Small talk makes her uncomfortable and, since she spends little time socializing with co-workers, "scheduled socials" are awkward. What's worse, the stress and anxiety literally make her sick.

Although it may not seem so, Jeri has the ability to change her experience. It starts with recognizing her feelings and implementing self-care to mitigate her challenges. Acknowledging she is an introvert who has social anxiety is a start. Here are a few other tools:

1. Share your feelings with your supervisor or a trusted colleague. Speaking your truth is empowering. You also open the door to receiving encouragement, professional development, and support.

2. In the days leading up to an event, establish a buddy system, and pair up with someone who can be your conversation partner.

3. Eliminate external stressors. Plan your outfit and your hair. Get important projects done well ahead of time before the event.

4. Manage your mind. This is difficult at first, as we are conditioned to imagine the feeling of something before it happens. In other words, we begin to feel anxious just thinking about socializing. Flip the script. Instead, visualize yourself feeling calm in the moment. Go back to that each time anxiety creeps up.

5. Do things that energize you. Identify the people or activities that fill your spirit or charge your emotional battery. Do those things or make those connections, so you are not fully depleted in social settings.

6. Create structure for yourself and set boundaries to reduce stressors. Going with a buddy is structure. Ride together or pick a meet-up time. Arrive early enough to take your time in choosing a seat. Strategize: Decide in advance if there will be people there you should make a point of connecting with and do it. Reward yourself. Plan in advance to give yourself some down time afterwards.

7. Take advantage of the times when you are most productive. I am a morning person. I am most productive during the day. I like to get the most important tasks done in the morning. As daylight fades, I feel less productive, or I must commit more energy and focus. I move tasks that require less brain energy to that portion of my day. This is important because it allows me to plan ahead for how I will accomplish my tasks as well as give myself grace when I know at this time of day, or in this particular environment, I'm really not at my best. There's no need to

force it. This is also where we must be honest with ourselves and those around us. Set expectations. There will always be something on the "to-do" list, but you don't owe an apology for expressing or addressing your needs while completing the task.

8. Take inventory of habits and behaviors. This was impactful for me. I recently noticed my habit of turning slightly to my right when talking with someone directly in front of me. From the perspective of the individual who was facing me, I wondered what they observed in my body language: How does my posture influence their perception of me or what I am communicating? I imagined what I would think if a person took that stance with me.

This habit goes back to how I adapted to having cerebral palsy, which underscores how my life experience influenced how far I leaned into my introversion. I wanted to hide my hand and the right side of my body where my muscles spasmed—my face, my neck, my right arm, and my hand. I don't know when I began shifting my body so that less of my right side was visible. Now, when I become aware of my awkward stance, I correct it in the moment.

Overcoming habits that don't serve you can be difficult. Sometimes you need the help and support of others. I did. Introverts tend to process and address these changes and feelings alone. Getting help or support requires vulnerability and transparency that is not intuitive. You may be surprised by the amount of freedom you feel when someone else helps you identify and release habits that limit your authentic self-expression.

I learned the value of cultivating a supportive community during a three-day conference in Atlanta a couple of years ago. Day one was a typical 8 a.m. – 5 p.m. schedule with breakout sessions and group activities. I was drained and exhausted at the end. I wasn't sure if I wanted to even begin days two and three. I really wanted to pack up and leave. I was overwhelmed by the experience. My only motivation to stay was the nonrefundable hotel room.

Part of why I wanted to leave was that I felt as if I didn't bring any value to the environment. I didn't feel seen or heard. It wasn't that I was being ignored. Among the hundreds of women, well-dressed, groomed, and polished, I felt small. Watching them interact with such freedom and confidence was intimidating. Contending with my mental dialogue about my shortcomings exhausted my energy.

On day two, I reluctantly headed down to the conference area. Women were already gathered in the outside lobby, socializing, taking photos, and basking in the women's empowerment energy. There among them was a woman about ten years older than me, who was documenting every day of her experience on social media. I loved her spirit. She was so full of joy, and she enthusiastically embraced everyone who came near. She called me over for a hug and said, "Let's do a live!"

I immediately pulled back, "No, I can't ..." I said almost panicking at the thought.

She did not allow me to finish my excuse. She grabbed both my hands, stood squarely in front of me, looked into my eyes, and said, "Don't you ever hide your hand again."

No one had ever told me that. No one had ever seen me that way or had the courage to call me out and up to where I belong. It was such a relief. I didn't realize I needed help and support. Her choice to be transparent and vulnerable gave me the courage to drop my defenses and allow myself to be exposed and vulnerable.

CHAPTER 5: STRATEGIES TO UNLEASH INNER POWER

From that moment forward, I practiced confidently displaying my full body and celebrating in how God made me. I'm sharing this in such detail because I want you to relate this to your own personal experience. Everyone has something that makes them feel inadequate, incompatible, unsafe, ugly, less appealing, or unworthy of what God has placed in your heart to do or to be.

Gary attended my "Unapologetic Introvert" webinar in January 2024, during which I shared my experience and similar strategies outlined in these chapters. He privately messaged me immediately after, saying how much the discussion had resonated with him and that he had taken many notes.

In February, Gary reached out again requesting a consultation. At our scheduled meeting, Gary was audibly exasperated. Voice trembling, he told his story:

Gary is an introvert, who after twenty years struggling with addiction, is celebrating six years clean and sober. He recently relocated from his hometown in Michigan to Santa Barbara, California, to reclaim his life. Gary spent his first months unhoused, eventually buying and living out of his car. He was thankful that after ten months, a Good Samaritan tapped on the car window and offered him a bed at a local shelter. Fourteen months in temporary housing—sharing space with other residents who were struggling in the lifestyle from which he was finally free—Gary was ready for stability.

He applied for low-income housing and was on the wait list to receive an apartment assignment through the local housing authority. However, as he witnessed several residents who applied after him receive their apartments, it looked like he'd been passed over. Gary reached out for help.

"I met all the qualifications and remained in compliance since arriving at the temporary housing, despite the challenges of living in a shared space," Gary said, in a frustrated tone.

When I asked how I could help, Gary said, "I need answers. I need help formulating my thoughts so that I make my point when I meet with the program staff and decision makers of the housing authority." Then, he confided how his twenty-year addiction had taken a toll on his body. A stroke in 2016, plus the physiological damage from the addiction, caused slurred enunciation, and his diction was imprecise. He stuttered while waiting for his brain and body to sync and deliver his thoughts.

"I felt like my ability to be precise, think, and speak clearly was a barrier to being taken seriously," Gary said.

Before his addiction, Gary had a promising career in commercial banking and, for a time, worked for the Federal Reserve.

"When given the opportunity for promotion, I lacked confidence," he said. "I was intimidated by upper management and feared that I was incapable of doing the job even though I was being trained for the next level and already doing some of the work. Consequently, I was bypassed for the promotion, and management selected someone of less seniority. The webinar helped me connect

CHAPTER 5: STRATEGIES TO UNLEASH INNER POWER

the dots. All these years, that's what I've been dealing with and not knowing."

For the next several hours we discussed his thoughts about the housing situation. I helped him narrow down the main points he wanted to communicate. I typed as he dictated. I emailed and texted his thoughts to him, and he immediately reached out to the housing authority and program managers. He emailed and texted all parties addressing his concerns. He took control by asking for follow-ups.

The next day, Gary informed me of his email and follow-up conversations with the housing authority management. The apartment representative reached out and assured him that he would be included in the next round of applicants to receive apartments.

"They were very apologetic and helpful in resolving the matter," Gary said.

We win every time we overcome our limiting beliefs and embrace our whole selves—the one-of-a-kind masterpieces of divine design that we are. Instead of giving up, Gary found his voice. He used his quiet power—problem-solving, critical thinking, and self-control—to advocate for himself. If nothing else, he had the courage to accept all the parts of his identity and show up for himself.

If we allow it, we will receive everything God has purposed for us to do and to be.

In May, Gary reported that he was living comfortably in his own studio apartment. He shared photos of his modest home with a small bathroom and a kitchenette that includes a cook top. A plant decorated the dining table that had seating for two. From the photos, I saw green grass within view of a mountain in Santa Barbara.

"It's ok that it's small," he said in a text message, "but it's mine."

Gary also reentered the workforce part-time. His confidence and passion caught the eye of an outreach worker who referred him for a position at a local nonprofit. Gary works as an Ambassador for the nonprofit, helping individuals who may be unhoused, need mental health or other support by conducting the initial intake and referring them to a caseworker to assist them in navigating the available resources.

Gary shared about a recent grand opening and fundraising event.

"As I pulled up to the event and saw the crowd of people including city officials, I thought about what we talked about," Gary said, referring to our sessions. "I thought about being an introvert and that we need to be more confident. I jumped out of my car, walked into the crowd, extended my hand, and said, 'Hello, my name is Gary.'"

I encourage you to assess yourself; and if you need support to move through challenges, it exists. Open yourself up to receive it, so you can become the best version of yourself. Determine if your habits and behaviors can be tweaked to achieve your desired goals.

CHAPTER 5: STRATEGIES TO UNLEASH INNER POWER

Simple actions like paying attention to your posture when you are speaking with someone can help you make a better impression. Are you looking them in the eye? Are you leaning in? Are you presenting a posture that says you are closed off, distracted, or tuned-out?

My go-to posture is to fold my arms across my torso. Many leaders, coaches, and experts in the communication field say folding your arms sends a visual cue that you are closed-off. For me, folding my arms is my way of hiding my spasms. I resolved this by searching YouTube for Power Postures and finding several that work for folded arms. I also found other positions to practice and add to my toolbox.

Another difficulty for me is making introductions because the standard is to lean forward and extend your right hand for that firm handshake. I can't do that because I don't have the fine motor control in my right hand. This seemed critical in the professional arena, as we're conditioned to the idea of making a strong first impression.

I'm still frustrated when encountering people who are unprepared or unwilling to make the adjustment. I have offered my left hand to shake and they insisted on reaching for my right, with a facial expression as if I didn't know the protocol. Once, I initiated a greeting by handshake and the young man refused to shake my hand at all, stating that he was taught to only shake with the right hand. My response, "Well, young man, you just missed an opportunity to learn an important lesson, that the world is not all black and white. People have different abilities. Sometimes you'll be forced to color outside the lines. The person who teaches you that lesson may not be as gracious as me."

A seasoned gentleman who overheard the conversation quickly pulled the young man to the side and offered the gentle correction he needed. While introverts are typically nonconfrontational, it was immensely freeing to be seen and heard in that moment.

I had to get over the uncomfortable aspects of that experience. One way of doing that is by accepting things you cannot control or change. None of that should impact your level of engagement, how you feel about what you bring to the table, and the values you have in yourself.

The last part of this strategy is to take time to reset. Reduce the chance of becoming overwhelmed in your environment. Know your limitations, and give yourself grace. This will require you to be vocal, set boundaries, and ask for what you need. This is critical in the professional environment. It would help so many employees if they felt comfortable telling their manager or supervisors what they need in order to be successful in performing their task, assignment, or role. Too often introverts suppress their feelings and ignore their needs. Fearing the stigma of presenting an introvert-related deficiency, we feel pressure to perform and over-perform repeatedly.

Practice quick, intermittent reset moments. For example, step away, take a break, take a breath, allow time and space for clarity, and to regain composure. Return with a refreshed mindset and confidence to fill your space in a manner only designed for you.

Strategy #2: Lean into the experience

Discomfort is unavoidable. Instead of becoming anxious in anticipation of or during an experience, lean into it.

CHAPTER 5: STRATEGIES TO UNLEASH INNER POWER

Accept the pull that leads you forward. Meaningful goals will require us to stretch outside of our comfort zone, and most certainly are achievable. You will find that pressing toward goals with the clarity that comes from self-awareness and self-acceptance will build your confidence and increase your capacity for more. Feelings of discomfort will soon be replaced with feelings of satisfaction with yourself and your accomplishments.

> I established a daily routine to leave my desk, go into team members' offices, and have genuine conversations. I know this seems simple and for many leaders, standard practice, but for introverts like me initiating conversation is neither intuitive nor preferred when you have work to do.

Awareness of habits and behaviors that negatively impact your goals allows you to take control of the situation to produce your desired outcome. Be intentional about serving your introvert preferences, while adding value to your environment.

For example, as a program director, my preference was to go directly to my office, focus on tasks that included everything from conducting staff meetings and giving performance reviews to planning a messaging campaign and writing a speech. My preference was to do the work and go home. However, I was a leader who was responsible for a team of not just workers, but individuals and their personality types and needs. I could not operate in my own preference alone with success.

I established a daily routine to leave my desk, go into team members' offices, and have genuine conversations. I know this seems simple and for many leaders, standard practice, but for introverts like me initiating conversation is neither intuitive nor preferred when you have work to do. It must be deliberate before it becomes routine and comfortable with practice.

When you go to work, make time to speak and greet your staff or co-workers. Look them in the eyes, express interest, and ask about their weekend. During these conversations, practice reciprocation. That means, when someone asks you, "How was your weekend?" you answer them with more than two words. Share a few details. If it was generally a good weekend at home, say something like, "I had a pretty good weekend, didn't do much but the weather was great, so I took my dog for a long walk." Then reciprocate. "How was your weekend?"

Seems obvious, and it is for many people. It wasn't for me. I assessed that I tended to answer those questions with a couple of words, little detail, and failed to reciprocate. As a result, it was a short conversation that added very little value to either party. On the other hand, giving a few details about yourself allows the receiver to know you better and connect with you on a deeper level.

Ask about their day. Ask about their weekend. Ask about their children. Talk about subjects that are interesting to them. These conversations are not for you to check the box. They must be genuine and meaningful. Establishing this rapport helps strengthen morale, encourages a trusting, supportive environment, and motivates your staff to become extremely loyal, hard

CHAPTER 5: STRATEGIES TO UNLEASH INNER POWER

workers. This is ground-level for building relationships and a game-changer for building a highly functional and performing team.

In social and networking environments, listen more than you talk. Ask open-ended questions, which allow others to share more about themselves. For example, "How did you like the [fill in the blank]?" or "What was your favorite part of the [fill in the blank]?"

As they elaborate, remember interesting details. The key to remembering is to find commonalities and share them at the appropriate pause in the conversation. Ensure your body language signals that you are paying attention. For example, look them in the eyes, smile, nod, and lean in naturally. For some introverts, this takes practice. You must become comfortable with yourself first.

People tend to gravitate to that energy. Smiling opens you up so that people sense that you are approachable. It draws in the people you are interacting with and encourages deeper conversation and the potential to strengthen relationships.

Be honest. Let people know upfront if you have difficulty remembering names. They will appreciate you letting them off the hook as well. It signals that you are honest and genuine.

For introverts, we spend more time inside of our heads. We process. We analyze. In those times, we are not fully present or in the moment. Practice being present.

Observe your environment. Are you at a large venue? Is it familiar to you? If not, what are some unique things about it? Are there people you know? Is there something of interest taking place? Look for things you can take away from the experience. Are there people of interest in the room? Perhaps this is an opportunity to make a meaningful connection. We'll discuss this more in-depth in Strategy #3 Seize the Opportunity.

Finally, have an exit strategy as part of your plan. Think about how you will enter and exit your environment. It doesn't have to be awkward. If you are at a social event and you've had enough, thank the host, and make your exit. Leave the setting guilt-free. Tell the truth. "I've had a long day. I have an early day tomorrow. I have to pick up my kid from soccer."

If you're in the work environment, in the office with staff or a co-worker and you've spent your allotted time in conversation, tell them that. Excuse yourself. "I have to get ready for an appointment."

Again, this is not new information, and you may be thinking, everyone knows this. If it wasn't intuitive for me, I'm willing to bet someone else is struggling. I struggled with feelings of exhaustion. I was done. I wanted out, and it took me way too long to figure out how to get in and get out gracefully.

Implementing these simple strategies structured my experience in a way that reduced my stress level. These strategies—be present, have meaningful conversations, build relationships—minimize feelings of guilt and the compulsion to over-perform.

Well-executed strategies help you develop confidence. Instead of avoiding an entire experience, set boundaries that will allow you to participate to your degree of comfort. The more I practiced it, I started to see the improvements in the quality of my interactions and the benefits of engaging people on a deeper level. I started to see the impacts of those simple adjustments.

CHAPTER 5: STRATEGIES TO UNLEASH INNER POWER

Strategy #3 Seize the opportunity

Have you ever attended a gathering and had little to no memory of the people you spoke with or what you talked about? Have you regretted missed opportunities? To seize the moment, you must be intentional, and you must manage your mind.

According to the Oxford English Dictionary, intention is the action of directing the mind or attention to something. In other words, we have the ability and, in my opinion, responsibility to direct our minds toward deliberate, purposeful actions and goals. We have more control than we take.

For example, in unfamiliar, overstimulating, or uncomfortable environments, introverts may retreat to their safe place—inside their heads. Consumed by our active minds, we are disconnected, less engaged with what is happening in the moment and in our environment. We miss occasions to have meaningful interactions and deepen relationships. We miss being fully present.

If you become aware of this tendency, take control. Identify and practice alternative behaviors. There are no perfect solutions, but there are multiple options from which to choose. Identify and test one or two, until you master them.

For example, instead of focusing on the dread of social interaction, identify a goal to accomplish while in the space. Consider your unique qualities, skill sets, and expertise and then focus your attention on delivering value to one person in the room. It could be something as simple as sharing the contact to a pet groomer with a new acquaintance. To get to that point, a conversation would have to take place in which you express more than two words. Set a time limit window to accomplish your goal, like within the first thirty minutes, so that you have a specific stopping point. These baby steps build confidence and strengthen your capacity to be okay in the room. Making purposeful connections is critical in family, social settings, and in the workplace.

Another baby step could be deciding ahead of time that you will approach at least three new people, introduce yourself, and ask open-ended questions until you discover one interesting thing about them. Building your comfort level in this arena can have many benefits.

Perhaps you'll meet someone you have been trying to connect with for months. Maybe you'll get a chance to close the loop or tie-up some loose ends with someone whom you've been corresponding via email. What if you are inadvertently introduced to someone you've been following on social media, or who you've admired but considered them outside your social reach, and you can finally get a burning question answered? Always consider when you are preparing to enter an environment, what is the value you can bring in that room and what value can you receive?

Shifting your thinking in this way disrupts old patterns of behaving that lead to stress and anxiety. Be inquisitive when engaging others. Be open to share differences and commonalities. By applying these strategies, you would not likely run out of conversation.

Be aware of tunnel vision, another habit that forced me to practice intentionality. In certain settings, I get so laser focused, I don't see what's happening in my peripherals. I miss side stories along the way. For example, when entering a crowded room, I'm on target to find and get to my seat. I don't see the people to my left and right. I

CHAPTER 5: STRATEGIES TO UNLEASH INNER POWER

move in such haste that the room is a blur. Once seated and looking around, I see that I missed opportunities to greet individuals whom I know or should get to know.

Another growth opportunity is overcoming fear of speaking in large or small group settings, in class, or in the board room. This seems simple, right? From my own experience, it is not. I needed to implement strategies to help me organize my thoughts and deliver them with clarity and precision. A big mental hurdle is overcoming our own self-talk. Conversations in my mind tell me that I am taking too long, nobody cares, and what if I am wrong.

This is where I have learned to engage my quiet power. You can, too.

We have meticulously prepared. We've done our primary and secondary research. We have expert knowledge of the subject-matter. We have note cards and bullet points. We practiced in front of a mirror. Now, slowly inhale deeply through your nose. Exhale, blowing through your lips. Be still. Be human. And deliver your words with confidence. Something as simple as taking a breath could make all the difference in your delivery.

I discovered this when I did public speaking early in my career. With a PowerPoint overhead, I stood in front of a crowded room that seated about 500 Soldiers with their commanding officers and delivered media engagement training in preparation for a unit deployment. All eyes on me, I spoke so quickly I barely took a breath between bullet points. I was operating out of sheer discomfort, as if the quicker I got to the last slide, the quicker I could get out of view. The feedback I received came from a friendly source, my daughter, who happened to be shadowing me that day, "Mom, you need to breathe when you talk."

Thankful for the feedback—that experience stayed with me throughout my career. It was one of several strategies I added to my toolkit along the way:

1. Treat it like a conversation. Use natural gestures.
2. Punctuation has a purpose. Use them as pause points—some longer than others.
3. Vary your tone and pitch to convey emotion and help emphasize key points.
4. Involve the audience by asking a question i.e. "By show of hands ...?"
5. Allow a few moments of awkward silence to draw in your audience.
6. Be human, laugh especially at yourself, when appropriate.
7. Pay attention to posture and facial expressions.
8. Don't read the slides verbatim. Speak from what you know.
9. Give examples, tell stories, and share anecdotes.

Sometimes, I still miss the mark. My words get jumbled. However, I released my concern about other opinions. My input has as much value as the next person. I don't own and cannot control anyone's reaction. I can control how deeply I allow other peoples' words to penetrate my sense of self-worth. I learned that I would much rather be heard, be actively engaged, and share my thoughts than leave the room feeling invisible. This realization was a huge growth moment for me.

Strengthening self-awareness also fortifies your ability to properly receive feedback. In other words, you have the ability to change what could be negative into a positive experience by receiving other comments as feedback rather than criticism. While it's another opinion, it's your choice to ascribe value to their words and whether or not

CHAPTER 5: STRATEGIES TO UNLEASH INNER POWER

to receive or ignore their input. Most importantly, their words do not become you, even if they inform you of something.

Self-assessment: You have the choice and the ability to step out of your box, to allow yourself to be fully present, visible, and engaged.

- Do any aspects of Jeri's experiences resonate with you? Under similar circumstances, what would you do differently?

  _____

  _____

  _____

- How confident are you with managing yourself in your environment?

  _____

  _____

  _____

- What are your go-to behaviors or practices in navigating uncomfortable spaces?

  _____

  _____

  _____

CHAPTER 5: STRATEGIES TO UNLEASH INNER POWER

- List 2 - 5 actions from Strategies 1 – 3 that you could implement immediately for your benefit.

  _____

  _____

  _____

  _____

  _____

  _____

Reflection: Personal experiences

- What personal accounts or experiences from Chapter Five resonated most with you? Why?

  _____

  _____

  _____

- Consider Gary's experience. At what point did he begin his self-assessment? What steps did he take to move forward? What was his breakthrough moment?

  _____

THE UNAPOLOGETIC INTROVERT

- Now, taking a similar approach, at what points have you experienced clarity, taken action, and achieved a breakthrough to show up for yourself rather than shrink back?

Chapter 6

The Blessing of Discomfort

"You gain strength, courage and confidence by every experience in which you really stop to look fear in the face. You are able to say to yourself, 'I have lived through this horror. I can take the next thing that comes along.' You must do the thing you think you cannot do."— **Eleanor Roosevelt, You Learn by Living: Eleven Keys for a More Fulfilling Life**

I remember thinking, *Is this what it feels like to thrive in discomfort?*

Something had changed for me. I was loving my introvert self and it showed. I began to see a difference in my interactions. I was mentally prepared and present at social gatherings. I moved around the room thoughtfully, entered and exited conversations easily while ensuring that I contributed something meaningful to the discussion. I was conscious of my body language and posture, although not compulsively. I felt fully in control of myself and confident in my presence.

I could see the results of doing my work, but I'll be honest, it didn't always stick. Sometimes, I slipped back into my old way of thinking and being. Lasting change requires diligence and giving yourself grace along the journey. It took many years to develop the behaviors that sabotaged my ability to be myself. I had to turn my energy toward releasing them. I started by examining my life experiences and how they contributed to my choices.

Living with cerebral palsy had a huge impact that I didn't connect with how far I leaned into introversion. Instead of designing a life that honored my abilities and values, I overcompensated by holding myself to unrealistic standards. In my mind, saying "No" to a work task was unacceptable. I was afraid of appearing inadequate. I was compelled to over-deliver, even when it meant working late and missing dinner with my family. I regret the years I judged myself harshly for making mistakes like calling someone by the wrong name or missing a meeting because I didn't see the late email about the time change. Sometimes, I beat myself up over extenuating circumstances, *How did I miss that email? If only I had spent more time on this task versus that? I need to get to work earlier.*

From the outside, I maintained a calm demeanor, but inside I was devastated, agonizing over the details of how a mistake occurred or where I failed to measure up. Under the surface of all of that was my inner narrative—I denied myself the experience of being human, setting boundaries, and asking for what I wanted and needed.

One of the first jobs I applied for after high school was a clerical position at a law firm in downtown Chicago. I arrived early for my interview and checked in at the receptionist window. "I type with one hand," I said confidently as I slid my application through the window to the lady completing my intake. I was ready for the next question, prepared to share my experience, and assure her

CHAPTER 6: THE BLESSING OF DISCOMFORT

that I was up to the task. I didn't get that far. She slid my application back through the window.

"We can't offer you the position," she said.

"I can do the work," I insisted.

She returned a firm, "No, we cannot offer you the position." That was the last time I disclosed my typing skills to an employer.

After college, I tried a different approach. I applied for a federal job and marked the box next to disability on the application. After reviewing my resume, the hiring official began to list types of positions that would be offered under that designation—laundry, custodial, and others of similar responsibilities—none in my field of study or within my qualifications. It was apparent that I was being matched to a job without a regard for my capabilities. I felt undervalued and my qualifications poorly assessed. I was hurt and disappointed. That was the last time that I disclosed to an employer that I had a disability. I eventually entered the federal workforce through a program that offered internships to recent college graduates based on academics and experience.

I buried these experiences and others like them in my introversion. The reality is instead of pushing them down or covering them up, they fed my story—the unspoken words that described what I thought of myself. *What if I make a mistake? What if I am not good enough?* It was easier to be quiet and stay in the background. I focused on my work and proving I belonged, even though my subconscious reminded me that I didn't.

I know now that when I feel embarrassed or anxious about something, to pause and check it against the truth of who I am today. Now, I tell myself that it's okay to make a mistake. There are no perfect people. I'm learning to stand in my truth, expressing my needs and setting boundaries for how and where I spend my energy. I hold myself accountable. When I have the urge to shrink back, I test it against my truth and step into the discomfort.

I challenge you to invest time in assessing yourself. The questions at the end of each chapter are designed to help you think deeply and discover your own truth.

Taking one at a time, examine your experience, the story you told yourself, or the story you accepted from someone else. Examine the truth in those words. But also, more importantly, examine the lie. Then, prepare to reframe your story and reshape your self-perception from the inside out.

Starting today by talking to yourself, re-tell the story of who you are and what you are capable of accomplishing. You must take action to move in the direction you want to go, because what you tell yourself is ultimately going to shape how you present yourself in any environment.

You have control. You have the ability to be a very strong presence. This requires self-awareness, a little practice, and a lot of courage, discipline, and commitment. You owe it to yourself to be your very best. You owe it to yourself to be heard. You owe it to yourself to get the most out of your personal and professional relationships. You owe it to yourself to starve the fear, which means don't allow it to reside in your mental space.

Instead, feed your mind by consuming resources that inspire self-love, self-acceptance, and courage. Enhance your confidence by taking action starting with baby steps. Action is important because it produces feedback. Now, let's pause. As we discussed in Chapter 5, resist the urge to receive feedback as criticism. Don't become distracted by

CHAPTER 6: THE BLESSING OF DISCOMFORT

the thought of making a mistake or being imperfect. Focus on what you can learn from feedback.

You can think all day long and pray all day long. You can want, meditate, and do all the things. Nothing will happen until an action takes place. That is a law. You must act in order for there to be some sort of reaction. That is your feedback. When received and used properly, feedback is invaluable.

Let's explore action steps. Choose something that aligns with your goals. For example, address the habit of tunnel vision or social anxiety. Start small. Test it out. Choose an activity that stretches you a little beyond your comfort zone. It could be the next time you purchase something at a full-service register, pause, look the cashier in the eyes, and say, "Hello." Ask them how their day is going.

This action step may seem simple, but it's not. Earlier, I described my habit of tunnel vision. I can get so deeply inside my own head that I'm oblivious to the world around me. If that resonates with you, imagine going to the grocery store, you barely notice the silver-haired couple in the produce isle or the new mom who is flustered and struggling to manage her two-year-old and her shopping list. An encouraging smile might have brightened their day. You didn't even see your co-worker when she passed by or maybe you did, and just wanted to avoid conversation. You missed opportunities to connect with people, to be present and in the moment, and to grow.

Simple steps outside your comfort zone build confidence. Allow feedback to generate positive energy. Pay attention to the momentum.

Momentum is a very sacred action because that is where you will get the most pressure to take your foot off the gas pedal. Don't do it. Fight through it. Just as there are two sides to a coin, there always will be a positive and a negative. You will receive unpleasant feedback. Take what is useful and discard the rest. You will feel pressure to ease back into your space of comfort. You will feel exposed and vulnerable.

You will have the urge to sabotage your progress, to skip a task, or to cancel a commitment you made to yourself. Easing up only feeds the old story about you. In those moments, lean forward and press in. You are at the cusp of a breakthrough. You are establishing new habits that align with your authentic self. I know this to be true because I've been there. On certain days, I am there. I share my story—my scars and my triumphs so that you can use them as guides on your journey.

Here's the thing: This is not a solo experience. It cannot be a solo experience. God did not create us to exist alone. We need community in order to excel. Number one, it gives us the opportunity to serve others. Number two, it puts us in spaces to be served and to receive support. As we fill others, others fill us. You won't experience the healing power of community if you isolate yourself.

Introverts prefer privacy. We are careful about who we spend time with. We are cautious about the details we share with others. We are guarded. Take this opportunity to grow.

If you only choose one person, find someone you trust to share with about your journey. If you're not ready for that, then start by listening to and reading the words of those who inspire you.

There are books, podcasts, YouTube channels, and blogs by people who have been through this process and surfaced on the other side. They are passionate about

CHAPTER 6: THE BLESSING OF DISCOMFORT

saying that you can do it, too. For nothing more than praise, receive affirmation that your introvert life has value. Use those people, let their experience serve your needs, and then eventually you will be able to live on the other side and serve someone else.

Self-assessment: Think about your life experience. Go beyond the fact that you have a temperament that leans toward introversion. What life experiences contributed to your personality preferences, behaviors, or habits?

_____

_____

_____

- What are the things you told yourself or others told you and that you believed?

  _____

  _____

- What experiences helped shape how you interact in your environment?

  _____

  _____

  _____

CHAPTER 6: THE BLESSING OF DISCOMFORT

- What are the things that embarrassed you, or that caused you to want to disappear?

　

- What caused you to feel like you failed, or that you didn't measure up?

　

- What decisions were made absent your voice? You just couldn't muster the words.

　

- What environments make you feel like you don't deserve to be present?

Reflection: The influence of others

- How often do you allow others to influence how you show up for yourself?
  _____
  _____
  _____

- After answering the questions above, did you identify any patterns of behavior that can be adjusted?
  _____
  _____
  _____

- Pick one "false" narrative and rewrite it to reflect the truth about you.
  _____
  _____
  _____

- How will you take control of your story going forward?
  _____

CHAPTER 6: THE BLESSING OF DISCOMFORT

_____

_____

_____

_____

_____

_____

_____

Chapter 7

Embrace your quiet power

"Let others lead small lives, but not you. Let others argue over small things, but not you. Let others cry over small hurts, but not you. Let others leave their future in someone else's hands, but not you."— Jim Rohn

If I may be completely transparent, it took many years for me to become confident in my own skin and to accept my whole body. Some days, I struggle more than others. There are parts of me that I love, like my honey-brown complexion and my brown eyes. I am grateful to have a loving family and friends who support and encourage me. Despite the many reasons to be full of joy, for a long time, I felt broken and ashamed. I was locked into an inauthentic identity. I was exhausted of holding up the wall, deferring to others, feeling invisible, and ignoring my instincts to live in my purpose.

Can you relate? I was so concerned with the expectations of others, my compulsion to prove that I was good enough, that I was numb to my own needs. I could barely hear my inner voice, "Stop playing small. You were designed to shine!"

God has a way of forcing us out of the spaces where we hide and ignore our truths. We are terrified when he

CHAPTER 7: EMBRACE YOUR QUIET POWER

strips away our distractions and excuses. After we have exhausted all options, we listen. When we are ready, our internal compass moves us forward one step at a time. We begin to feel relief as each forward step draws to us the resources we need to continue. Before long, a sense of urgency replaces doubt, as we explore and expose every aspect of our personality.

In the year leading up to writing this book, I pushed myself outside of my comfort zone. I leaned into life in ways I never imagined. Every step forward was an opportunity to learn more about myself and to face my fear of exposure, rejection, and embarrassment.

One of my most impactful opportunities to stretch and grow was during an eight-month executive leadership program. The program, designed to give community and business leaders an in-depth view of the socio-economic aspects of our city and county, also included typical networking and team projects. I was ready to test my quiet power. From Day 1, I decided to follow an alumni's advice, "The time goes by faster than you think. Get the most out of every experience." I chose to lean in.

The first teambuilding exercise was an outdoor excursion at Adventureworks park in Tennessee. My team scaled a thirty-three-foot pole called The Quantum Leap. Each team member earned points based on how far up they scaled the pole. I watched as my teammates strapped into the harness, clicked on the helmet, and ascended the pole. First up, my firefighter teammate climbed the pole like routine training. He made it all the way to the top earning the maximum points for our team. By his example, reaching the top might be challenging, but was definitely achievable.

Then, the founder of a local nonprofit stepped forward. Trembling, she strapped in and started her ascent. We all cheered her on from below, guiding her to the pegs that gave her leverage to step up and pull up. Back on the ground, we celebrated how far she was able to go. The height she reached was impressive. She also earned us points.

A couple more volunteers took their turn, then it was my turn. Heart in throat, helmeted, and harnessed, I began to scale the pole. I had no concept of what it meant to pull up my body weight. This was the first physical activity I'd done in nearly forty years. As I began to ascend the pole, placing my feet on the pegs and pulling up, left hand and then right hand, thoughts filled my head. This was September, only three months since my stroke. I was grateful to get to do this, that the second stroke did not leave me debilitated, and that my body was cooperating.

The gentle cheers and encouraging words from my teammates filled me with emotion. I felt their energy as if willing me to the top. I heard their words, "Keep going. You can do this. I'm so proud of you." I moved upward left hand, pull up, right hand, pull up. Right hand. Grip tight. Right hand. Spasm. Then fear. I didn't know if I could trust my spastic right hand to grip the peg long enough to release my left hand and allow me to reach up for the next peg.

In that moment, I heard myself say the words, "I can't."

My team encouraged gingerly, "You can do this, Brendalyn. We got you," as they guided me to pegs that I could use to leverage my body weight with my feet.

When the words slipped through my lips again, "I can't," my teammates gently began to help me down. My

CHAPTER 7: EMBRACE YOUR QUIET POWER

feet touched the ground as my teammates expressed cheers and congratulations. The emotion of the moment was palpable. I was so proud that I made the attempt. At the same time, I wondered if I could have gone farther, if I gave up too soon. The second those two words, "I can't" passed through my lips, I felt like the nine-year-old little girl and was disappointed that her feelings of "I'm not good enough" were still there. I thought I had long since healed that wound.

When you start tapping into your authentic self, old limiting beliefs are less palatable. I vowed to push myself harder. On the next occasion, we visited a military installation and were invited to rappel from a thirty-four foot tower, on which 101st Airborne Division Soldiers trained to earn their Air Assault badge. I paid close attention to the soldiers giving instruction and demonstrating the proper technique. I watched as my classmates stepped into harnesses, donned helmets and gloves, and ascended the stairs to the tower platform. They each approached the platform edge, knelt to lock their rope into their harness, stood, and after instructed, stepped off the platform and descended.

Again, I took my turn. In full gear, I climbed the fifty-seven stairs. On top of the platform, my legs were like jelly, my heart palpitated, and I felt weak as if I would pass out. Taking the stairs back down was not an option. I didn't give myself the satisfaction of looking back. I noticed a classmate who was struggling to approach the tower's edge.

"Let's do this together!" I exclaimed. We both went to our positions. I knelt to lock in the rope.

"Stand up," the soldier said. "Now, turn backward." With nothing but the rope around my waist, locked into the harness, and refusing to look down, I kept my eye on the soldier guiding me. When instructed, I stepped off the wall and descended the tower. The rush of adrenaline and exhilaration as my feet touched the ground was beyond words.

In my fifteen-second decent, I released decades' worth of "... what if I can't do it? ... what if I make a mistake? ... what if I'm not good enough?"

In the past, I would have talked myself out of attempting both of these challenges. They were too risky, too exposed, and too much potential for embarrassment. But now, I'm learning to show up as my full self, unapologetically introverted, and free of shame.

The truth is embracing your introversion is a bold declaration that you're no longer willing to hide or apologize for who you are. It's a commitment to living life on your terms. And, when you grant yourself permission to be authentically you, you open the door for others to do the same.

It takes courage to stand in our truth, and we must desire the same for others. We must celebrate diversity of thought, ability, and personality. We must recognize that our differences are what make us stronger together.

> **The truth is embracing your introversion is a bold declaration that you're no longer willing to hide or apologize for who you are. It's a commitment to living life on your terms. And when you grant yourself permission to be authentically you, you open the door for others to do the same.**

CHAPTER 7: EMBRACE YOUR QUIET POWER

Let's redefine introversion and acknowledge the power it represents. While we thrive in spaces that provide solitude and reflection, we also shine brightly among the greatest achievers, inventors, leaders, and legends. Our skills and abilities deliver value and make a difference in our families and workplaces.

I challenge you to question your story while examining the beliefs and habits that keep you boxed in. Showcase your quiet power by celebrating the human experience that you were not created to live small. You are enough and the world needs your deep thinking, wise counsel, careful analysis, and humble strength.

Self-assessment: Have you unlocked your authentic self?

- Under what circumstances do you express your authentic self guilt-free?

  _____

  _____

- What are the thoughts, fears, or beliefs that prevent your genuine self-expression?

  _____

  _____

- In which areas of your life do you feel most inhibited?

  _____

  _____

  _____

CHAPTER 7: EMBRACE YOUR QUIET POWER

- What tool(s) could you implement from previous chapters to help you break free of your inhibitions?

  _____

  _____

  _____

- Absent any limitations—fear, limiting beliefs, etc.—list 2-4 things that you would do?

  _____

  _____

  _____

  _____

Reflection: Your quiet power

- In the context of Chapter Seven, what does quiet power mean to you?

  _____

  _____

  _____

THE UNAPOLOGETIC INTROVERT

- In what ways have you leveraged your quiet power to fully express yourself?
  _____
  _____
  _____

- Share one past event or experience in which, given the chance, you would use your quiet power differently?
  _____
  _____
  _____

- Share an instance where you chose to stand out and shine on your terms? How did you feel in that moment?
  _____
  _____
  _____

Chapter 8

Dear Introvert: Fill your space unapologetically

"The privilege of a lifetime is to become who you truly are."— Carl Jung

I see you suffering in silence, navigating a world that is designed and oriented for extrovert personality traits. I know the struggle, contending with the chatter inside our heads and inner world, while fulfilling our responsibilities in the outer world. Depending on the environment or the experience we burrow deeply in thoughts, *Is this the thing I should be doing? Is this right for me? Is this my purpose? Do I belong here? Am I good enough?*

These questions may go unanswered because we lack clarity about our 'who' and our 'why.' *Who* we are is tied to what we do, our preferences and our lifestyle. Our *why* refers to our inspiration. It's the conviction that gets us out of bed each day, compels us to choose the hard right over the easy wrong, and calls us to risk personal or financial peril to achieve greater for ourselves and others.

Michael Jordan, an introvert, is one of the greatest basketball players to ever play the game. That's *who* he is, but *why* he is one of the greatest basketball players to ever play the game is because of the disappointment he faced when he was rejected on his Junior Varsity basketball team. And as a result, that experience created an insatiable drive within him to be the best ever. His drive permeated throughout his entire basketball career.

In the autobiography, *Rosa Parks* (Penguin Random House, 2005), historian Douglas Brinkley, details how, in 1955, the African American seamstress changed history when she refused to surrender her seat to a White passenger on a segregated bus in Montgomery, Alabama. Her courageous defiance triggered the Montgomery Bus Boycott and signaled the beginning of the Civil Rights Movement. Rosa Parks is described as "shy, self-effacing, soft-spoken and averse to crowds."

Because of her quiet leadership, Rosa Parks is esteemed among highly regarded leaders who challenged human, social injustice including Eleanor Roosevelt, Mahatma Ghandi, Dr. Martin Luther King, Jr., and Nelson Mandela, all introverts. Remembered today as a historic figure, the mother of the Civil Rights Movement, we are most familiar with her *who*. She worked as a seamstress and volunteered to serve as Secretary for the NAACP chapter.

Brinkley takes us deeper into her *why*, and the well-documented accounts of her life. Parks, born and raised in rural Alabama in 1913, had witnessed innumerable injustices and atrocities leveled upon human beings simply because of race.

She lived in terror in the Jim Crow era south, choosing to stay up with her father as he guarded their home at night with a loaded rifle.

She fought alongside her husband, Raymond Parks, a Charter member of the NAACP, to free eight young Black

CHAPTER 8: DEAR INTROVERT

men sentenced to death in 1931, after being convicted of raping two White women on a freight train in Alabama.

She experienced life in which White supremacists sabotaged the 15th Amendment by murdering hundreds of Black Americans for voting, running for office, or taking leading roles in their communities.

"This powerful form of intimidation was the norm throughout the south," Parks said.

Heaped on top of the terror were other forms of oppression. Blacks were excluded from juries, denied access to public libraries, hired only for menial jobs, prohibited from enrolling in universities, and denied access to public libraries and parks.

She first encountered Montgomery bus driver James F. Blake, in 1943 on her way to register to vote, entering the front of the city bus that was already full in the rear of Black passengers.

Blake, wearing a pistol on his side, promptly ordered her to get off the bus and re-enter the rear. Parks knew that Blake had a reputation of pulling away, leaving Black passengers on the side of the road after they paid their fare to enter the rear. Upon her refusal, Blake attempted to physically escort her off the bus, to which Parks demanded not to be touched.

She would disembark on her own, but not before letting her purse fall to the floor and sitting in the "whites only" seat as she bent down to pick it up. Parks vowed to never ride Blake's bus again.

Until the day in 1955, twelve years later, she mistakenly boarded Blake's bus. Parks' *why* changed history. A woman of deep Christian faith, Parks was never one to back down. When the time came, she chose her seat, and she filled it.

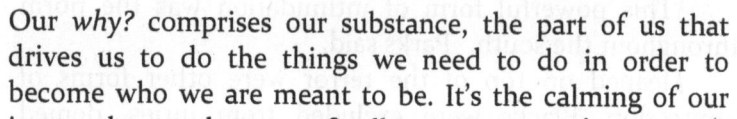

Our *why?* comprises our substance, the part of us that drives us to do the things we need to do in order to become who we are meant to be. It's the calming of our inner chaos when we finally stop resisting and just do it. The long hours of laboring, practicing, perfecting, and mastering a thing fulfilled. We see the failures changed into opportunities, setbacks turned into set-ups, and giving up transformed into giving back. The *why?* guides the work we do on ourselves, for ourselves, out of the spotlight, absent the cheers and external validation. Our *why?* is the source of tears welling in our eyes, the lump in our throats, the quiver in our lips, the humility in our spirit, and an ineffable feeling of wholeness when our authentic *who* appears.

> **My assignment in writing this book is to help you pull back the layers and uncover your *why*, to express your value, and unleash your quiet power. You belong to an esteemed tribe.**

My assignment in writing this book is to help you uncover your *why*, to express your value, and unleash your quiet power. You belong to an esteemed tribe. We've explored the research. While extroverts tend to focus externally, introverts are better able to engage their imagination for strategic professional and personal use. While extroverts are thinking about the now, introverts are thinking about what could be.

Introverts are epic storytellers, artists, musicians, scriptwriters, authors, and actors. Because they spend more time in their heads, they more readily tap into their subconscious, and actively engage their creativity.

Whereas extroverts are energized by external forces, they don't necessarily spend enough time with themselves examining their beliefs, dreams, feelings, and emotions. Introverts have a natural, neurological aversion to overstimulation. We are wired to be more connected to our feelings, emotions, subconscious, and imagination.

Some of the most important works in human history were conceived by introverts. Whether we refer to Picasso or Mozart or the framers of the Constitution, Benjamin Franklin or Alexander Hamilton, most of these people are known introverts. Their ability to exist and thrive outside of an overly stimulating world set them apart and gave them a distinct advantage. Introverts have a unique ability to shut it off and shut it down, a quality extroverts may desire more of at times.

"Introverted people who balance their energy have perseverance and the ability to think independently, focus deeply, and work creatively."—Olsen Laney

That is not to say that all extroverts are addicted to overstimulation and have neither imagination nor creative ability. Both history and science disprove that theory. At the same time, both history and science support the theory that introverts have innate sensitivity, which has better equipped us to engage with our feelings and emotions, to engage our mental space and formulate well-thought out opinions.

Introverts possess very unique skill sets that cause them to produce exceptional results. They are Warren Buffett, Arianna Huffington, Bill Gates, and Steve Jobs. There are many still unnamed, hiding among us today. Are you one of them? If so, this is your time.

Susan Cain writes, "If you are an introvert, find your flow by using your gifts. You have the power of persistence, the tenacity to solve complex problems and the clear-sightedness to avoid pitfalls that trip others up; you enjoy relative freedom from the temptations of superficial prizes like money or status, indeed your biggest challenge may be to fully harness your strengths."

It's time for you to peel back your layers and expose your true yourself. Your purpose can only be fully realized in authentic self-expression. Attempts to suppress your individuality; to assimilate into a particular group, culture, or environment; or to compare yourself to others negatively impact your sense of wholeness and well-being. However you lean on the spectrum of introversion to extroversion and personality traits, you have the ability to deliver value.

On my journey, understanding my introversion and my personality traits was empowering. I gained confidence by knowing my *why*. I reclaimed control and my ability to choose how I wanted to show up for myself, my family, and the people I serve. I discarded my mask. I surrendered the "extrovert persona" that I had adopted at the expense of my own needs.

I accepted responsibility for the box I had built and the walls I erected. I embraced myself as the courageous nine-year-old little girl who stayed in a safe space for so long that she had neither the tools nor the capacity to free herself. As an adult, she didn't recognize the triggers that

CHAPTER 8: DEAR INTROVERT

caused her to shut down and retreat to her safe space rather than lean into her unique qualities and trust her divine design. Today, I recognize that accepting other peoples' perceptions of me, their words, or their uninformed feedback kept me fastened securely inside.

I wonder how many of your choices influenced how you maneuver inside and outside of your boxes. What could you have done differently? What do you wish you had the courage and confidence to try?

I'm grateful for all of my experiences. They were valuable life lessons that guided me to, first, peer through the crack, then break the seal, and finally step outside my box. I gained perspective as I learned more about where I fall on the spectrum of introversion to extroversion and how my preferences impact my decisions and the environments in which I am most comfortable. Now, I see myself differently. I focus on the positive aspects of my personality and my value. I pay attention to my preferences and the quirks of my personality that make me special. Instead of suppressing them, I make space for them.

For example, when triggered to withdraw and shut down, I listen to my body. I assess my circumstances, and I thoughtfully choose my response. My reactions are less automatic, and the result is deliberate effort to use education, tools, and resources that help me show up more authentically for myself from the inside out.

In closing, I pray the words on these pages will inspire you to speak up, step forward, take the challenge, and ask for the promotion. Most of all, that you choose to live your best life. Never again apologize for the unique qualities of your personality. Let them shine bright, and allow them to serve you and those around you. You are thoughtfully designed. There won't ever be another, and only you can fill your space.

Kudos for letting others see and experience you. Thank you for allowing me to be part of your journey.

Unapologetic Introvert

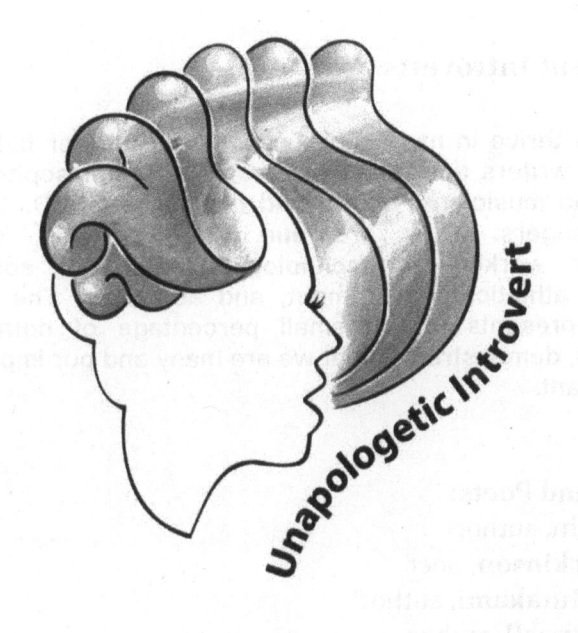

Prominent Introverts

Introverts thrive in myriad professions and career fields. They are writers and poets, scientists and philosophers, artists and musicians, actors and filmmakers, CEOs and world-changers. They are our family, friends, and neighbors working in technology, healthcare, social services, athletics, government, and academia. The list below represents just a small percentage of notable introverts, demonstrating that we are many and our impact is significant:

Writers and Poets:
Susan Cain, author
Emily Dickinson, poet
Haruki Murakami, author
George Orwell, author
J.K. Rowling, author
Dr. Seuss, author, aka Theodore Seuss Geisel

Scientists, Philosophers, and Spiritual Leaders:
Charles Darwin, naturalist
Albert Einstein, physicist
Mahatma Gandhi, spiritual leader
Soren Kierkegaard, philosopher and theologian
Dalai Lama, (Tenzin Gyatso), spiritual leader
Isaac Newton, physicist and astronomer
Eckhart Tolle, spiritual teacher and author

PROMINENT INTROVERTS

Artists, Musicians, Actors, and Filmmakers:
Adele, singer-songwriter
Halle Berry, actress
Beyonce, singer and songwriter
Frédéric Chopin, composer and pianist
Courteney Cox, actress
Johnny Depp, actor
Vin Diesel, actor
Bob Dylan, singer-songwriter
Aretha Franklin, singer and songwriter
Morgan Freeman, actor
Lady Gaga, singer and actress
Anne Hathaway, actress
Audrey Hepburn, actress and humanitarian
Janet Jackson, singer and actress
Nicole Kidman, actress
Keanu Reeves, actor
Shonda Rhimes, author, producer, and screenwriter
Ed Sheeran, singer-songwriter
Steven Spielberg, filmmaker
Meryl Streep, actress
Barbara Streisand, actress and singer
Vincent van Gogh, painter
Emma Watson, actress

Business Leaders:
Brenda Barne, former Sarah Lee CEO
Sara Blakely, Spanx Founder
Warren Buffett, Berkshire Hathaway CEO
Bill Gates, Microsoft co-founder
Wendy Kopp, Teach for All CEO/co-founder
Debra Lee, former BET CEO

Marissa Mayer, Sunshine CEO and former Yahoo CEO
Larry Page, Google co-founder
Gwyneth Paltrow, Goop Founder
Charles Schwab, Charles Schwab Corp founder/co-chairman
Nina Vaca, Pinnacle Group Founder/CEO
Susan Diane Wojcicki, Former YouTube CEO
Mark Zuckerberg, Facebook co-founder and CEO

Historical Figures and Leaders:
Queen Elizabeth II, Queen, United Kingdom, 1952-2022
Laura Bush, U.S. First Lady, 2001-2009
Thomas Jefferson, Third U.S. President, 1801-1809
Dr. Martin Luther King, Jr., Minister, Civil Rights leader
Abraham Lincoln, Sixteenth U.S. President, 1861-1865
Nelson Mandela, First South African President, 1994-1999
Barak Obama, 44th U.S. President, 2009-2017

Personality Tests

Below are personality tests commonly used to assess introversion, extroversion, or other personality traits. They are accessible online and, as indicated, several are free.

The list provided is for informational purposes only, does not endorse any particular test, and their selection and use reflect personal choices to be approached with discretion. Readers are advised that:

1. No personality test is universally accurate or applicable to all situations.

2. Results from these tests should not be used as a substitute for professional advice.

Myers-Briggs Type Indicator (MBTI) – One of the most popular personality assessments, identifying 16 personality types based on preferences in four dichotomies: Extraversion (E) vs. Introversion (I), Sensing (S) vs. Intuition (N), Thinking (T) vs. Feeling (F), and Judging (J) vs. Perceiving (P). **There is a cost with this assessment.** https://www.mbtionline.com/

All of the following assessments are FREE:

Big Five Personality Test (OCEAN) – Measures five major dimensions of personality: Openness to Experience, Conscientiousness, Extraversion, Agreeableness, and Neuroticism. https://www.truity.com/test/big-five-personality-test

16 Personality Factor Questionnaire (16PF) – Assesses 16 primary personality factors, including one that measures introversion vs. extraversion.
https://openpsychometrics.org/tests/16PF.php

HEXACO Personality Inventory - Expands on the Big Five by adding a sixth dimension: Honesty-Humility. The other dimensions are Emotionality, Extraversion, Agreeableness, Conscientiousness, and Openness to Experience.
https://hexaco.org/

16 Personalities (based on MBTI) – Provides insights into your personality type based on the Myers-Briggs Type Indicator (MBTI). https://www.16personalities.com/

Open Extended Jungian Type Scales (OEJTS) – Based on Carl Jung's theory of psychological types and provides a free alternative to the MBTI. https://personalityprobe.com/

Personality Test Center – Offers various free personality tests, including a Jungian type test and a Big Five test.
https://www.personalitytest.net/

Humanmetrics Jung Typology Test – Based on Jung's and Briggs Myers' typology, this test provides insights into your MBTI personality type.
https://www.humanmetrics.com/personality

Bibliography

Numerous works explore the topic of introversion. Below are the authors, experts, and thought leaders who have guided me on my personal journey. These individuals have significantly contributed to our understanding of introversion. Through their research, writing, and advocacy, they help reshape societal perceptions and empower introverts to leverage their strengths.

Their words resonate deeply with me, and they will remain my trusted companions as my journey unfolds. I provide this list for your information and to give proper credit to the individuals referenced in this book. However, I encourage you to conduct your own research. Find the voices that speak to you and choose your own companions in self-development:

Douglas Brinkley, historian:
Rosa Parks (Viking, 2000)

Susan Cain, author and speaker:
Quiet: The Power of Introverts in a World That Can't Stop Talking (Crown, 2012)
Bittersweet: How Sorrow and Longing Make Us Whole (Crown, 2013)

Sophia Dembling, writer and journalist:
The Introvert's Way: Living a Quiet Life in a Noisy World (Tarcher Perigee, 2012)

Jenn Granneman, author:
The Secret Lives of Introverts: Inside our Hidden World
(Skyhorse Publishing, 2017)

Steve Friedman:
"10 Survival Tips for Introverted Leaders"
https://introvertdear.com/news/10-survival-tips-for-introverted-leaders/

Laurie Helgoe, Ph.D., psychologist and author:
Introvert Power: Why Your Inner Life Is Your Hidden Strength (Sourcebooks, 2008)

Jennifer B. Kahnweiler, Ph.D., executive coach and speaker:
The Introverted Leader: Building on Your Quiet Strength
(Berrett-Koehler Publishers, 2018)

Marti Olsen Laney, Psy.D., psychotherapist and researcher:
The Introvert Advantage: How Quiet People Can Thrive in an Extrovert World (Workman Publishing, 2002)

Brian R. Little, Ph.D., psychologist and professor:
Me, Myself, and Us: The Science of Personality and the Art of Well-Being (Public Affairs, 2014)

Michelle Obama, First Lady, 2009-2017, Advice for girls battling self-doubt.
https://www.youtube.com/watch?v=bzNke_GYGHg&t=316s

About the Author

Brendalyn Carpenter Player is an Unapologetic Introvert on a mission to transform quiet nature into a superpower. Her journey to personal freedom uniquely qualifies her to guide others in embracing their authentic selves.

Living with cerebral palsy since childhood, Brendalyn understands firsthand the challenges of feeling different and the power of self-acceptance. She has transformed her own experience of releasing debilitating thoughts of brokenness into a beacon of hope for others. Through life's challenges and triumphs, Brendalyn rewrote her mental narrative to proclaim, "I can. I will. I belong, and I am more than good enough."

Brendalyn's professional background adds depth to her insights. As a retired Army Civilian, she leveraged over 20 years of strategic communication experience in high-energy, fluid environments. As the Director of Public Affairs at Fort Campbell, Kentucky, one of the largest U.S. Army installations, Brendalyn led a team serving the information needs of a 200,000 soldier, family, civilian workforce, and retiree population. Her achievements range from facilitating high-level media engagements during Presidential visits to managing crisis communications after natural disasters and pivoting public affairs operations during the COVID-19 pandemic.

While adapting to dynamic work environments became second nature, Brendalyn experienced the stress of constantly being "on." She credits exceptional mentors, her work ethic, and personal development for her career success. "Among the important lessons I learned were how to assert myself when necessary and the value of embracing solitude to recharge," she shares.

Now, as the owner of Brendalyn Player Communications and Unapologetic Introvert Founder, Brendalyn offers a safe space for individuals to assess their communication strengths and challenges. She shares tools and strategies that inspire courage and foster tangible results in both personal and professional lives. Her approach encourages fellow introverts to lean into discomfort, honor their needs, and stand firm in their authenticity.

Brendalyn's message is clear: Introversion is not a deficit but an invaluable strength. For CEOs, mid-career managers, dedicated team members, and everyone in between, she provides a roadmap for living authentically—be it standing out boldly or delivering your best performance from behind the scenes.

Are you ready to discover your quiet strength and make your introversion your greatest asset? Connect with Brendalyn to begin your journey of authentic empowerment.

Visit https://unapologeticintrovertspace.com/ to learn how you can work with her and unleash your introvert superpower.

THE UNAPOLOGETIC INTROVERT

Milton Keynes UK
Ingram Content Group UK Ltd.
UKHW021052131124
451151UK00009B/130